William Anderson

A brief biographical sketch of the medical profession of Indiana county

William Anderson

A brief biographical sketch of the medical profession of Indiana county

ISBN/EAN: 9783741135446

Manufactured in Europe, USA, Canada, Australia, Japa

Cover: Foto ©ninafisch / pixelio.de

Manufactured and distributed by brebook publishing software (www.brebook.com)

William Anderson

A brief biographical sketch of the medical profession of Indiana county

A BRIEF
BIOGRAPHICAL SKETCH
—OF THE—
MEDICAL PROFESSION
—OF—
INDIANA COUNTY, PENN'A, AND

The First and Second Sanitary Reports, and Papers on Sclerosis of the Nerve Centres, Pyemia, Nervous Diseases, Bacteria, Tobacco and Hygiene.

BY WILLIAM ANDERSON, M. D.,

Member of The Indiana County Medical Society, permanent member of Medical Society of the State of Pennsylvania, permanent member of The American Medical Association, member of the Inter-National Medical Congress, and member of The Inter-Continental American Medical Congress.

TIMES STEAM PR.NT, INDIANA, PA,

PREFACE.

At a meeting of The Indiana County Medical Society in May, 1890, I was appointed to prepare and read a brief biographical sketch of the Medical Profession of Indiana County. Pa., at the meeting in September. When the Society heard my sketch a number of the members expressed a desire to have my paper published, I solicited a short delay for the purpose of correcting the original manuscript, and now it is offered to the profession; aware of many imperfections. It is well known that accurate records are seldom kept in any department of society in the United States. In some parts of the world you will find records of all the transactions of churches, schools and families, but it is not so in this country. The American people as a rule are not recorders, are not historians. This state of society is so well known at the present day that it is not necessary for me to point it out. In 1880 I hastily collected a sketch of the Medical Profession for Captain Armes for his history of Indiana County, and now I offer the members of the Medical Profession a more accurate sketch. My present history covers ninty years, and as far as I know, I am the only person that has been pressed into such an unpleasant task. And now my retrospect is finished, and in closing the work assigned me, I am conscious of the anxiety of many of the younger members of the profession to learn something about the organization of the County Medical Society, and also the publication of some of the papers read at an earlier date than their entrance into the profession. To gratify them I have added a few papers on medical subjects, hoping my associates will contribute similar papers.

W. A.

BIOGRAPHICAL SKETCH OF THE MEDICAL PROFESSION OF INDIANA COUNTY

BY

WILLIAM ANDERSON, M. D.

At a meeting of the Indiana County Medical Society I was appointed to prepare a biographical sketch of the Medical Profession of Indiana county. As many of you are aware Indiana county was formed from Westmoreland and Lycoming counties by Act of Assembly, passed March 30, 1803, and the county seat located in 1805, and the first county officers were elected in 1806. I am aware of the many difficulties connected with the work assigned me, when I know that for a period of near eighty years, the Medical Profession of Indiana county was without a history; or any permanent record of their names; and many of them were not permanently settled. Under such circumstances, I am conscious; that with all the care and caution I can take, to do justice to all, I will be severely criticised and censured. In summing up the history of the Medical Profession of Indiana county, I observed that a number of them practiced their profession in different parts of the country. In order to make my sketch more convenient, I will give every physician's history, principally at his first place of settlement in the county, and as I pass on through the towns and villages *alphabetically*, will only mention date and period of location at that place.

Dr. Samuel Talmage was the first physician of whom we have any history, to practice medicine in the territory that now belongs to Indiana county. He was born in Massachusetts and educated there. He had training in a Medical College as he frequently mentioned to his family, that an epidemic of yellow fever prevailed in a hospital, where he prosecuted his studies, and his experience with that disease.

Before 1800 there were only four Medical Colleges in the United States: the University of Pennsylvania, at Philadelphia; Columbia College, New York; Harvard, Mass., and Dartmouth, New Hampshire. There was an epidemic of yellow fever along the Atlantic coast in 1793, and another epidemic of the same disease in 1797 and 1798. We are not able to tell which of these epidemics he referred to when speaking of his experience with yellow fever. He undoubtedly came to Pennsylvania soon after he served in the hospital, for he practiced medicine east of the Allegheny mountains before he came to Newport. Was married to a widow lady whose maiden name was Ann Fry, of Dauphin county, Pa. He moved to Newport, Indiana county, about 1800, (at that time Westmoreland county.) His practice extended over a large field on both sides of the Conemaugh river. Sometimes he visited the scattered families that lived near where the town of Indiana now stands, before the county was organized or the county seat located. When Dr. Talmage settled at Newport, the surrounding country was full of howling wolves, which made night travel dangerous. He made several narrow escapes returning from professional calls.

About 1810 he moved to the west side of the Conemaugh river opposite the Broad Fording. Here he kept tavern and practiced medicine. Shortly after he located here, he discovered a salt spring in the middle of the river. When the river was low, cattle and deer would go in and drink, and lick the boulders, where the water oozed up. The doctor sank a vessel, the shape of a barrel and puddled it, to shut off the river water and dipped up the water and ran it out in wooden spouts, and boiled it in large iron kettles, and made the first salt on the Conemaugh river. Salt at that time was selling for five dollars per bushel. Dr. Talmage moved from Broad Fording in 1826 or 1827 to Bogg's Salt Works, one and one-half miles above Apollo, on the Westmoreland side of the Kiskiminetas river. Then moved to Oldtown, at the mouth of Pine Run in the same county. Here he lived and practiced his profession until 1847. Always had an interest in salt works from the time he discovered the salt water in the middle of the river, until he moved from the State, and practiced medicine at the same time. He had gained a good reputation in Obstetrical practice, and was frequently called a considerable distance from home in difficult cases. His wife died in 1844. In 1847 he went to Fishing Creek, Tyler county, West Virginia, and lived with his son-in-law, William Robison, until his death in 1853, aged 88 years.

William Johnston sank a well by boring for salt water in 1813. He reached salt water at the depth of 450 feet. This was the first salt well above Saltsburg.

Dr. Reed, a Westmoreland county physician, occasionally visited families on the north side of the Conemaugh river before there were permanently settled physicians in the county. His visits were mostly in the neighborhood where Blairsville now stands.

Dr. George Hays, a native of one of the New England States, where he received his education, literary and medical, located in the county of Indiana, about the time of its organization. He boarded with Gen. Campbell, near Campbell's Mills, on Blacklick creek, for a number of years, and with a Mr. Repine of the same neighborhood, and at a latter date with Joseph Turner, one mile east of Jacksonville. His practice extended over a large and sparsely settled territory, from Cambria county on the southeast to Armstrong county on the west. After spending a number of years in Indiana county he moved to the neighborhood of Greensburg, Westmoreland county, and practiced his profession there until his death.

ARMAGH is the oldest living town in Indiana county at present. It was laid out in September, 1792, on a road that led from Frankstown, on the Juniata river, to Pittsburgh, Pa. It is 18 miles west of Ebensburg, Pa., and 14 miles east of Blairsville, Pa., we have very little history of the first physicians in Armagh. Dr. John Young was the first. Dr. Vanhorn succeeded Young, and Dr. Andrew Getty was the next physician. As to their early history or date of location we have no data.

Dr. Robert K. Scott, came from the eastern part of the State in 1812, and practiced his profession there until about 1824, and moved to the place where Georgeville now stands, practiced there a few years and then moved to Mercer county, Pa.

Dr. Samuel F. Devlin, a native of Ireland, came to this country at an early age; was educated partly by private tutors. Studied medicine with Dr. E. P. Emerson, located in Armagh in 1818, and practiced his profession there until a short time before his death. He died in the vicinity of Armagh in 1842 or 1843.

Dr. Frank Young, a son of Hon. John Young, of Greensburg, Westmoreland county, Pa., after a thorough preparatory education, studied medicine and settled in Armagh shortly after Dr. Devlin located there, and practiced medicine there several years. He then went to Scotland and remained there until his death. Dr. Young was a man of more than ordinary literary attainments. After he settled in Scotland he became a member of a number of the most learned scientific societies in that country.

Dr. John Hay, a native of York, Pa., where he was educated and studied medicine, located in Armagh about 1828 and practiced his there profession about ten years, then moved to Johnstown, Pa., and practiced his profession there until his death.

Dr. William G. Stewart, a native of Brushvalley township, Indiana county, Pa., was educated at the Common Schools and Indiana Academy. Studied medicine with Dr. James M. Stewart, Indiana, Pa. Graduated at the Jefferson Medical College, Philadelphia. Located in Armagh in 1839, and practiced there until his death in 1851.

Dr. George W. Gettys, moved from Indiana to Armagh in 1838 and practiced there one year, and returned to Indiana. (See Indiana.)

Dr. William Altman, a native of Indiana, was educated at the Indiana Academy, studied medicine with Dr. J. M.

Stewart, Indiana, Pa. Graduated at Jefferson Medical College, Philadelphia, and located in Armagh in 1847. Remained there about one year, then moved to Punxsutawney, Jefferson county, and practiced there until 1853; moved to Indiana and practiced there until the early part of the year 1854, and returned to Punxsutawney and remained there until his death, March 20th, 1890. Dr. Altman was one of the Surgeons of the 28th Reg't, Pa. Vol. He was Associate Judge in Jefferson county one term and member of the Legislature from same county from 1885 to 1888.

Dr. *Crawford Irvin* was born in Blair county, (then part of Huntingdon,) April 20th, 1824, graduated at Jefferson College, Cannonsburg, Pa. Studied medicine with Dr. J. A. Landis, Hollidaysburg. Graduated at Jefferson Medical College, Philadelphia, Pa., 1847. After practicing a few months in Davidsburg and Johnstown, he came to Armagh and practiced there until 1849, then moved to Frankstown, Blair county, and practiced there until 1854, then moved to Hollidaysburg, where he is practicing his profession to present time.

Dr. *A. Jackson Clark*, a native of East Wheatfield township, Indiana county, Pa., was educated at Armagh, studied medicine with Dr. William G. Stewart. Graduated at Jefferson Medical College, Philadelphia, in 1849, located the same year in Armagh and practiced there a few years, then moved to New Florence, Westmoreland county, Pa., and continues to practice his profession there.

Dr. *Samuel F. Stewart*, a native of Brushvalley township, Indiana county, Pa., was educated at the Blairsville Academy. Studied medicine with his brother, Dr. William G. Stewart. Attended a course of lectures at Jefferson Medical College, Philadelphia. Located in Armagh in 1850 and practiced there until his death in 1857.

Dr. *Wm. D. McGowan*, of Westmoreland county, after a thorough preparatory course, studied medicine. Graduated at the Medical Department of the University of Pennsylvania in 1851. Located in Armagh the same year and practiced his profession there about one year. Then retired from the practice of medicine for a number of years, engaging in other business in Pittsburgh, Pa. Then returned to Philadelphia and reviewed the course of medical instruction and is now practicing his profession in Ligonier, Pa.

Dr. James D. McClure moved from West Lebanon to Armagh in 1853, and practiced his profession there until the fall of 1854. (See West Lebanon.)

Dr. Robert J. Tomb, a native of East Wheatfield township, Indiana county, Pa., was educated at a Select School, near Greenville and at the Indiana Academy. Studied medicine with Dr. James Taylor, in West Fairfield, Westmoreland county, Pa. Graduated at Jefferson Medical College, Philadelphia in 1854. Located in Armagh the same year and is engaged in the practice of medicine in the borough of Armagh until the present time. Dr. Tomb entered the United States service as Assistant Surgeon in 1862. First in the Second Reg't Vol. Infantry, and then Surgeon of 193 Reg't Pa. Vol. Was mustered out the at close of the war and returned to his home and continued his practice.

Dr. Robert Barr was born in Green township, (now Cherryhill) Indiana county, Pa., August 20th, 1828. He was raised on a farm, attended the Common School in the winter until the spring of 1846, when he entered the Cherrytree Academy and remained there during the summer, taught school the following winter, then attended a Select School near Greenville, then a term at the Indiana Academy. Studied medicine one year with Dr. Wallace B. Stewart, of Greenville, and finished his course of study with Dr. Thos. St.Clair. Graduated at Jefferson Medical College, Philadelphia, in 1854. The same year he entered into partnership with Dr. Samuel F. Stewart in Armagh, and continued in partnership until the death of Dr. Stewart in 1857. He remained in Armagh until 1860, and moved to Indiana, and remained there until his death, March 2, 1882. In 1861 Dr. Barr was appointed Surgeon of the Sixty-seventh Reg't, Pa. Vol. After serving in that position 18 months he was appointed Division Surgeon, which position he held until his term of service expired.

Dr. *Benjamin F. Tomb*, a native of East Wheatfield township, Indiana county, Pa., was educated in Armagh. Studied medicine with his brother, Robert J. Tomb. Graduated at the Western Reserve Medical College, Cleveland, Ohio, in 1867. Located at Chest Springs, Cambria county, Pa. Remained there two years, then moved to Armagh and practiced there a few years, then moved to Mechanicsburg and remained there twelve years. In 1885 he moved to Morrellville, near Johnstown, Pa., and is practicing there at present.

Dr. *George M. Gamble* moved from Cherrytree to Armagh in 1859 and remained there one year, then returned to Cherrytree. (See Cherrytree.)

Dr. *Wallace B. Stewart* moved from Greenville to Armagh in 1859, and practiced his profession there until his death in 1875. (See Greenville.)

Dr. *Andrew Johnstown*, an old practioner of Hollidaysburg, Blair county, Pa., moved to Armagh late in life, and practiced there a few years. He died there in 1876.

Dr. *J. McCurdy*, a native of Indiana county, was educated at Blairsville. Studied medicine with Dr. M. L. Miller, of Blairsville. Attended a course of lectures. Located at Big Run, Jefferson county, Pa., in 1870, practiced there a few years. Moved to Parnassus, Westmoreland county, Pa., remained there a year and in 1875 moved to Armagh and remained there about a year and moved to Dravoesburg, Allegheny county.

Dr. *A. J. Souther and Dr. Crawford* located in Armagh a number of years ago, but did not remain long in the place. They did not get into practice there. No history of either.

Dr. *Theodore F. Klages*, a practioner from Pittsburg, Pa., located in Armagh in 1891, and resides there at present. He is a graduate of the Nashville Medical College, Tennessee, in the class of 1881.

AVONMORE—*Dr. William Frederick*, the first physician in Avonmore, is a native of Westmoreland county, was born and raised in the vicinity of Parnasus; educated and studied medicine in that place. Graduated at the Western Pennsylvania Medical College, Pittsburgh, Pa., in 1888; located in Avonmore the same year and is practicing his profession in that place until the present time.

BELLS MILLS in the vicinity of Blacklick Station, was laid out in 1848.

Dr. Thomas McMullen, a native of Center township, Indiana county, Pa., was the first settled physician in the place. He was educated at the Common Schools and Blairsville Academy; studied medicine with Dr. James McMullen, in Mechanicsburg. Graduated at the Jefferson Medical College, Philadelphia. Located at Bells Mills in 1853, and practiced his profession there until the fall of 1854, when he moved to Mechanicsburg and in 1856 to Monmouth, Illinois; and remained part of a year in that place and returned to Mechanicsburg, then moved to Greenville in 1858 and practiced his profession there until his death, February 12, 1884. Dr. McMullen was a member of the Indiana County Medical Society, from its organization, and member of Medical Society of the State of Pennsylvania since 1865. He represented Indiana county in the House of Representatives of Pennsylvania during the years 1872-73.

Dr. T. P. Simpson came from Beaver county to Bells Mills for manufacturing purposes about 1870. After spending a short time in the place the community pressed him sometimes to visit patients. After serving them a few years, he moved to East Liberty, Allegheny county, Pa.

Dr. Samuel L. Wiggins was raised in the vicinity of Shelocta, Indiana county, Pa., and was educated at the Common Schools and Elderton Academy. Studied medicine with Dr. Thomas J. Marlin. Graduated at Jefferson Medical College in 1873, and located in Livermore, Westmoreland county, Pa., the same year, and in 1875 moved to Blacklick Station, and remained there until the fall of 1885, then moved to Philadelphia, and in 1886 to McKeesport, Allegheny county, Pa., where he resides at present. Dr. Wiggins was a member of the Indiana County Medical Society, while he lived in the county, and is a member of the Medical Society of the State of Pennsylvania.

Dr. Joseph M. Kerr, a graduate of the Medical College of Ohio, at Cincinnati, after practicing several years in Allegheny county, Pa., located at Blacklick Station in the fall of 1885, and practiced there until June, 1888, then he moved to Brushton, Allegheny county, Pa.

Dr. David P. Jackson moved from Greenville to Blacklick Station in June 1888, and practiced his profession there until July, 1891; then moved to New Bedford, Lawrence county, Pa. (See Greenville.)

Dr. Andrew A. Johnston was born in Armstrong county, Pa., October 13th 1854. His early life was spent on a farm; was educated at the Common Schools, Plumcreek Normal School and Atwood Academy. Studied medicine with Drs. Duff and McAdoo, of Atwood; graduated at Western Pennsylvania Medical College, Pittsburgh, Pa., in 1891. Located at Blacklick Station, July, 1891, where he is engaged in the practice of his profession.

BLAIRSVILLE was laid out in the fall of 1818, the brush was partly removed in 1819.

Dr. Edward P. Emerson was the first physian in Blairsville. He was a native of Ireland and received his education, literary and medical, in his native country; and then emigrated to the United States and located first at Ebensburg, Cambria county, Pa., where he practiced his profession for a few years, then moved to Indiana county and located at Campbells Mills, on Blacklick creek, where he practiced over a large district of thinly settled country at that day. He boarded with General Campbell when he first came to the county, and at a later period at a hotel that stood where Smith's Station is at present on the Indiana Branch railroad. While at this place the town of Blairsville was laid out, and he moved there in 1820, and practiced his profession there until his death in 1861. Dr. Emerson stood high professionally.

Drs. Simmons and Craighead located in Blairsville in 1820, and practiced medicine in partnership for a short time, then moved away. We have no reliable history of these physicians.

Dr. Duffield located in Blairsville in 1827 for the purpose of practicing medicine. He died there in 1828.

Dr. Robert J. Marshall, a native of Franklin county, Pa., was educated at the Academies of Cumberland, Md., and Chambersburg, Pa. Studied medicine with Dr. John Boggs, of Greencastle, Franklin county, Pa. Attended lectures at Jefferson Medical College, Philadelphia. Settled in Blairsville in 1827 and continued to practice his profession in the same place until his death, April 13th, 1891, after 64 years practice of medicine.

Dr. Gillespie located in Blairsville a short time after Dr. Marshall, but did not remain long.

Dr. Samuel P. Brown, more recently of Greensburg, Pa., practiced a short time with Dr. Emerson.

Dr. John Gilpin, a native of Maryland, where he received his preparatory education; studied medicine with Dr. Emerson. Attended lectures and practiced medicine a short time in Blairsville. He then moved to Kittanning, Pa., where he practiced a number of years; then moved to Punxsutawney, Jefferson county, Pa., in 1849, and practiced there a few years; then moved to Cecil county, Md., and in a short time to California and died there about 1867.

Dr. Andrews settled in Blairsville about 1840, only remained a short time. (No history.)

Dr. Robert Montgomery Smyth Jackson, a native of Huntingdon county, Penn'a, and graduated at Jefferson College, Canonsburg, Pa. Studied medicine and graduated at Jefferson Medical College, Philadelphia, in 1838. He practiced his profession a few years in Huntingdon and Blair counties; then moved to Blairsville, Indiana county, Pa., in 1842, where he practiced his profession until 1852, then moved to Cresson and took an active part in making that place a health resort in the summer season, and remained there until 1861, when he entered the army as Surgeon of the Twenty-third Regiment, Pa. Vol., and was afterwards appointed Medical Inspector of the 23d Army Corps, and at the time of his death was acting Medical Director of the Department of Ohio. He died at Chattanooga, Tennessee, January 28th, 1865. He was a member of the Pennsylvania Geological Commission, American Philosophical Society, and Academy of Natural Sciences.

Drs. Hammell and Gemmill located in Blairsville about 50 years ago; only remained a short time in the place.

Dr. Isaac William Wiley was born at Lewistown, Mifflin county, Pa., March 29th, 1825, and was educated there; studied medicine and graduated at the Medical Department of the University of New York. In 1846 he came to Blairsville and practiced medicine with fair success until 1850; then went to China as a Medical Missionary and remained in China until 1853, his wife died and he returned to the United States. From 1854 until 1858 he filled a pastorate in New Jersey; and then for 15 years was Principal of a Seminary and Editor of the *Ladies' Repository* of Cincinnati, Ohio. In 1872 he was elected Bishop of the Methodist Episcopal Church. Twelve years later, while on an Episcopal tour, he visited the Mission which he had founded in Foochow, China, and died there in November, 1884, in the house in which he resided as a missionary in 1852.

Dr. McKim, a native of the Juniata Valley came to Blairsville in 1848, and was associated with Dr. Jackson for a short time; then returned east. He was a graduate of the University of Pennsylvania.

Dr. Fundenberg, of Westmoreland county, Pa., located in Blairsville about 1848. In a short time he moved to Somerset, Pennsylvania.

Dr. Martin L. Miller, a native of Indiana county, studied

medicine with Dr. Emerson; graduated at Franklin Medical College, Philadelphia, Pa., in 1848; located in Blairsville the same year, and has continued the practice of his profession in the same place until the present time.

Dr. Campbell, a practioner from Huntingdon county, Pa., settled in Blairsville about 1850; but moved in a short time to the neighborhood of Greensburg, Pa., where he died.

Dr. Anawalt, now of Greensburg, spent a short time in Blairsville before he located in his present situation.

Dr. T. M. Laney practiced his profession in Blairsville from 1853 to 1865. (See Georgeville.)

Dr. Terrence J. Cantwell was raised at Blairsville; was educated at the Blairsville Academy; studied medicine with Dr. Emerson; graduated at the University of Pennsylvania. Settled in Youngtown, Westmoreland county, Pa., in 1845, and practiced his profession there until 1854, then moved to Blairsville and practiced there until his death in 1865.

Dr. Frank M. McConnoughey, a native of Westmoreland county, Pa., graduated at Jefferson College, Canonsburg, Pa. Studied medicine with Dr. James McConnoughey; graduated at the Jefferson Medical College, Philadelphia; located at West Newton, Westmoreland county, in 1846; practiced his profession there a few years, then moved to Chillecothe, Ohio, and moved to Blairsville in 1862, and practiced his profession there until 1873, then moved to Mount Washington, Allegheny county, then to Greensburg, then to Wilkinsburg, next back to Blairsville, then to Mount Pleasant, Westmoreland county, where he resides at present. He was a membrr of the Indiana Medical Society from 1862 until 1873.

Dr. William R. Spear practiced medicine 23 years in New Alexandria, Westmoreland county, Pa., then moved to Warrenton, Missouri, then returned to Blairsville, Indiana county, Pa., about 1860, and in 1870 moved west. He was more or less engaged in the practice of medicine while he resided in the county.

Dr. John W. Hughes, a native of Punxsutawney, Jefferson county, Pa., was educated at the Common Schools and Glade Run Academy; studied medicine with Dr. Johnston, of Punxsutawney. Graduated at the Cincinnati College of Medicine and Surgery in 1861. Located in Leechburg, Armstrong county, Pa., and practiced there about two years; then moved to Blairsville and remained there until 1884; then moved to Latrobe, Westmoreland county, where he resides at present. Dr. Hughes held the position of Assistant Surgeon of the Fifth Regiment of Pa. Cavalry for two years.

Dr. S. R. Rutledge is a native of Westmoreland county, was educated at the Common Schools, Select Schools and Eldersridge Academy. Studied medicine with Dr. Banks, of Livermore and Dr. Anderson, in Indiana. Graduated at Jefferson Medical College, Philadelphia. He was associated with Dr. Banks, of Livermore, in the practice of his profession for eighteen months; then located at Palmersville, Allegheny county, and in a short time moved to Mansfield, and in July, 1871; then moved to Blairsville, where he has been regularly engaged in his profession to the present time. Dr. Rutledge is a member of the Indiana County Medical Society, and of the Medical Society of the State of Pennsylvania and of the American Medical Association, and has been Surgeon for the Pennsylvania Railroad Company for the last 17 years.

Dr. Luther S. Claggett is a native of Montgomery county, Md., was educated at the Common Schools and St. Timothy's Hall, near, Baltimore City. Studied medicine with Drs. Claggatt & Walls, of Baltimore City. Attended lectures at the University of Maryland, in Baltimore. Graduated at the Long Island College Hospital, Brooklyn, New York in 1868 and the Jefferson Medical College, Philadelphia, in 1877; he located at Penn Station, Westmoreland county, in 1868, and remained there eight years, and in 1877 he moved to Blairsville and has been regularly engaged in the practice of his profession there to the present time. Dr. Claggett is a member of the Indiana County Medical Society, and Medical Society of the State of

Pennsylvania, and of the American Medical Association.

Dr. *Isaac N. Leyda*, after a regular college course, studied medicine; graduated at the University of Pennsylvania in 1876; located in Blairsville the same year and remained there near two years, then moved to Manor Station, Westmoreland county, Pa., where he is engaged in the practice of his profession at the present time.

Dr. *I. P. Klingensmith* was born near Jeannette, Westmoreland county, Pa., April 18, 1850. Was educated at the Common Schools and Academies in his native county, and finished his preparatory education at the Capital University, Columbus, O. He commenced the study of medicine with Dr. Kamerer, of Greensburg, Pa., and finished with Prof. S. W. Gross, of Philadelphia. Graduated at the Jefferson Medical College, Philadelphia in 1875. Located at Derry Station, Westmoreland county in 1873, and practiced his profession there for eight years, and moved to Blairsville in 1883, where he resides at present. Dr. Klingensmith has been Surgeon for the Pennsylvania Railroad since 1876. He is a member of the Indiana County Medical Society, Medical Society of the State of Pennsylvania, The American Medical Association, International Medical Congress and many other societies.

Dr. *William Hunter* was born in Philadelphia. Was raised at Greensburg, Pa.; was educated at the Greensburg Academy: studied medicine with Dr. Spronger, (Homeopathist); graduted at the Homeopathic Medical College, Cleveland, Ohio, in 1864; he located in Greensburg, but in a short time moved to Blairsville where he resides at present.

Dr. *Archabald Falconer* setteled in Blairsville several years ago, claiming that he had passed through a thorough course of medical instruction in London, England, but failed to obtain a diploma, but had twenty-six years experience in practice of medicine. He remained in Blairsville and vicinity until his death in 1886.

Dr. *A. Edgar Tussey*, a native of Stone Valley, Huntingdon

county, Pa.; was educated at a Classical School in his native county, and at the Normal School, Indiana, Pa.; studied medicine with Dr. John C. Barr, Huntingdon county; graduated at the University of Maryland, at Baltimore. He located in Blairsville in 1883, and moved to Stone Valley in 1884, and a few years later to Baltimore and is now in Philadelphia.

Dr. George Hunter was born in Idaville, White county, Indiana; was educated in his native State; studied medicine with Dr. William Hunter, of Blairsville; graduated at the Hahnneman Medical College, Philadelphia, Pa., in 1886. Located in Indiana the same year, and practiced there a part of a year, then moved to Blairsville where he resides at present.

Dr. Albert T. Rutledge, a native of Livermore, Westmoreland county, Pa., where he was educated; prepared for entering a Medical College in Johnstown; attended two courses of lectures at Toledo Medical College, Ohio; graduated at Jefferson Medical College, Philadelphia, in 1889; located in Blairsville the same year, and continues to practice in the same place to the present time. Dr. Rutledge is a member of the Indiana County Medical Society.

Dr. Elisha P. Swift, a native of Allegheny City, where he received a good Common School education and took a full course at Lafayette College, Easton, Pa. After graduating he had the degrees of A. M., and A. B., conferred on him; studied medicine with Dr. Robert B. Mowry, of Allegheny City, and finished his course of study with Dr. I. P. Klinginsmith; graduated at the University of Pennsylvania in 1889; located in Blairsville the same year and practiced his profession there until the fall of 1890; he moved to Florence, Wisconsin. Dr. Swift joined the Indiana County Medical Society shortly after he settled in Blairsville.

Dr. John B. Carson is a native of Elderton, Armstrong county, Pa.; was born April 18, 1866; was raised in Saltsburg; was educated at the Saltsburg Public Schools, Saltsburg Academy and Normal School, Indiana, Pa.; studied medicine with his father, Dr. Thomas Carson; graduated at Jefferson Medical College, Philadelphia, in 1889; located at Niles, Ohio, remained there a few months, then moved to Blairsville where he is engaged in regular practice.

Dr. *James Leslie Harding* was born in Pittsburgh, Nov. 7, 1860; moved to the vicinity of Blairsville in 1864; was educated at the Blairsville Academy and State Normal School, Indiana, Pa.; studied medicine with Dr. Banks, at Livermore; graduated at Starling Medical College, Columbus, Ohio, in 1883; located in Pittsburgh, Pa., and practiced there seven years; then moved to Blairsville in 1890. While in Pittsburgh Dr. Harding was surgeon for Penn'a. R. R. for four years and city physician two years.

CENTERVILLE was laid out in 1828.

Dr. *Liggett*, a native of Scotland, was the first physician in Centerville. He received his literary and medical education at the University of Glasgow, Scotland. He came to the United States and located in Centerville in 1842, and practiced medicine there until the summer of 1846, he returned to Scotland and died in Glasgow the following winter.

Dr. *Joseph McBreth*, a native of Brushvalley township, Indiana county, Pa.; was educated at the Indiana Academy; studied medicine with Dr. James M. Stewart; attended a course of lectures at Jefferson Medical College; located in Centerville in 1848 and practiced there about one year, then moved to Galena, Ohio.

Dr. *James Taylor*, a native of Wheatfield township, Indiana county, Pa.; was educated at the Blairsville Academy; studied medicine with Dr. Emerson; graduated at the Jefferson Medical College, Philadelphia; located in Centerville in 1849 and practiced there a few years; then moved to West Fairfield, Westmoreland county, Pa., and is practicing his profession there until the present time.

Dr. *William Caldwell*, a native of Indiana borough, where he was educated. He was engaged in publishing a paper for several years in Blairsville; he retired from editorial work and studied medicine with Dr. Johnston, of Punxsutawney; attended a course of lectures and located in Centerville in 1853, and practiced medicine there about a year, then moved to Blairsville and engaged in the drug and apothecary business for a few years; then moved to Johnstown, Pa., and engaged in the mercantile business.

CHERRYTREE was laid out in 1840.

Dr. *William A. Piatt*, a native of Lycoming county, Pa., was educated at the Williamsport Academy; studied medicine with Dr. Thomas Lyon, of Williamsport; graduated at the Jefferson Medical College, Philadelphia; located at Cherrytree in 1848, and practiced medicine there until 1855, then moved to Vinton, Benton county, Iowa, and remained there one year, and returned to Cherrytree and continued to practice his profession there until his death in 1860. Dr. Piatt was a member of the Indiana County Medical Society and was the first settled physician at Cherrytree.

Dr. *Joseph H. Ake*, practiced medicine at Cherrytree from 1853 to 1855. (See Gettysburg.)

Dr. *George M. Gamble*, a native of Susquehanna county, Pa., was educated at Harvard College; studied medicine with Dr. George F. Horton, of Terrytown, Bradford county, Pa.; graduated at the Jefferson Medical College, Philadelphia; practiced in his native county a few years; then located at Cherrytree in 1855, and practiced there until 1859; then moved to Armagh and practiced there a year; and moved to New Milford Susquehanna county, Pa. Dr. Gamble became a member of the Indiana Medical Society shortly after he located at Cherrytree.

Dr. *R. A. Lorelace*, a native of York, York county, Pa.; where he was educated and studied medicine with Drs. Fuget and Nebinger; attended lectures at Jefferson Medical College; located in Lewisburg, York county, and practiced there about five years.

He moved to Cherrytree in 1856, and practiced his profession there until 1869; he moved to the state of Indiana and returned to Cookport in 1870; and in a short time moved to Cherrytree and practiced there until 1878; then moved to Pine Flat and in 1880 returned to Cherrytree and remained there until 1889 then moved to Williamsport, Lycoming county, Pa., where he is at present.

Dr. James Kelly, moved from Taylorsville to Cherrytree in 1859 and practiced there two years, and moved to Pleasant Unity, Westmoreland county, Pa. (See Taylorsville.)

Dr. James T. Adair, settled at Cherrytree in 1861 and practiced about a year in that place. (See Indiana.)

Dr. Adam C. Wassam, a native of Indiana county, was educated and studied medicine in Darke county, Ohio; graduated at the Cincinnati College of Medicine and Surgery; located at Cherrytree in 1867 and practiced his profession there until 1873; then moved to Eureka, Kansas; and is in Wachita, Kansas, at present.

Dr. Emanuel Brallier, a native of Cambria county, Pa., was educated in Ebensburg; studied medicine with Dr. Bunn; graduated at the Jefferson Medical College, Philadelphia, Pa., located at Cherrytree in 1868, and practiced his profession there until 1879 when he moved to Chambersburg, Franklin county, Pa., and continued to practice there until his death. Dr. Brallier was a member of the Indiana County Medical Society, and of the Medical Society of the State of Pennsylvania.

Dr. William Hosack, moved from West Lebanon to Cherrytree in 1879, and practiced there about three years. (See West Lebanon.)

Dr. Joseph U. Blose, a native of North Mahoning township, was educated at Glade Run Academy, studied medicine with Dr. J. Wilson Morrow; graduated at Columbus Medical College, Ohio; located at Cherrytree in 1881, and practiced there until 1886; when he moved to Altoona, Blair county, Pa., where he resides at present. Dr. Blose was a member of the Indiana County Medical Society, and of the Medical Society of the State of Pennsylvania.

Dr. James Calvin Miller, a native of South Mahoning township, was educated at Plumville select school and Glade Run Academy, studied medicine with Dr. McEwen in Plumville graduated at the Jefferson Medical College, Philadelphia, located at Cherrytree in 1885, and continues his professional work there until the present time.

Dr. George Martin, moved from Kimmell to Cherrytree in 1886, and practiced his profession there until 1888. (See Kimmel.)

Dr. Norris Cameron moved from Greenville to Cherrytree in 1888 and practiced there until Feb. 1881. (See Greenville.)

Dr. James Curry Shook, a native of New Washington, Clearfield county, Pa., where he was raised, educated and studied medicine with Dr. Rice, of Hastings, Clearfield county, Pa., graduated at the Jefferson Medical College, Philadelphia; in 1881 located at Cherrytree, Indiana county, Pa., where he resides at present.

CLARKSBURG was laid out in 1841.

Dr. Samuel M. Ogden, a native of Westmoreland county, Pa., was educated at Eldersridge Academy and Jefferson College, Cannonsburg, Pa. Studied medicine with Dr. James Taylor; graduated at Castleton Medical College, Vermont; located in Clarksburg in 1851, but did not remain long; he went to California, and spent a few years there then returned and settled in Latrobe, then moved to Ohio—returned to Pleasant Unity and died very suddenly. He was the first physician in Clarksburg.

Dr. James H. Bell, a native of Westmoreland county, Pa., was educated at the Blairsville Academy. Studied medicine with Dr. Blackburn, of New Derry; graduated at Castleton Medical College, Vermont; located in Clarksburg in 1852, and practiced there until 1856; then moved to Eldersridge and remained there untill 1861; then moved to Butler, Pa.; and engaged in the drug and apothecary business, and in 1868 moved to Blacklick Station, and engaged in general mercantile business.

Dr. Bolinger, a physician from Armstrong county, moved to Clarksburg; only remained a short time; moved to Illinois.

Dr. John S. McNutt, moved from Georgeville to Clarksburg in 1864, remained a short time and then moved to Apollo. (See Georgeville.)

Dr. Thomas J. Marlin, a native of Washington township, was educated at a select school at Kellysburg and Glade Run Academy; studied medicine with Dr. Robert McChesney; graduated at Jefferson Medical College, Philadelphia; located in Clarksburg in 1867; remained there until 1869; then moved to Shelocta and practiced medicine there until February, 1889; then moved to Tarkio, Atchison county, Mo., where he resides at present. Dr. Marlin was a private soldier during the late war. He was a member of the Indiana County Medical Society.

Dr. Bruce L. Calhoun, a native of Armstrong township; was educated at a select school in their district at Parkwood; studied medicine with Dr. Virtue; attended lectures at the Cincinnati College of Medicine and Surgery; located in Clarksburg in 1869, and practiced there about a year, then moved to Parnassus and more recently to Verona.

Dr. R. M. Orr, was born in Armstrong township; studied medicine with a brother in the State of Indiana; located in Clarksburg and remained there about a year; then moved to Mercer county, Pa., and died about eight years ago.

Dr. Alexander M. Rea, a native of Washington county, Pa.; where he was educated and studied medicine, graduated at Jefferson Medical College, Philadelphia; located in Clarksburg, did not remain long in the place, then moved to Atwood, Armstrong county, and from there to West Middleton, Washington county, Pa., where he resides at present.

Dr. William B. Walker, was born in Wayne township, Armstrong county, Pa. in 1851; educated at the common schools and

Dayton Academy; studied medicine with Dr. Sharp, of Dayton; graduated at the Cincinnati College of Medicine and Surgery; located in Dayton, Armstrong county, in 1876, and practiced his profession there until the fall of 1884; then moved to Clarksburg, Indiana county, Pa., where he resides at present.

COOKPORT was laid out in 1858.

Dr. Alexander Hamilton Allison, a native of East Mahoning township, Indiana county, Pa., was born June 6, 1842; was educated at Dayton and Glade Run Academies; studied medicine with Drs. McEwen and Ansley; attended lectures at the Jefferson Medical College, Philadelphia, Pa.; located at Cookport in 1866 and practiced his profession there until 1877, when he returned to his early home and in 1880, located in Marion Centre where he resides at present.

Dr. Abram R. Lorelace, settled in Cookport in 1870, and practiced his profession there for a short time. (See Cherrytree.)

Dr. John N. Evans, a native of Ebensburg, Cambria county, Pa., where he was educated; studied medicine with Dr. A. P. Field; graduated at the American Eclectic College, Philadelphia; located in Carrolltown, Cambria county, Pa in 1871, and then moved to Ebensburg in the same county; moved to Cookport in 1876, practiced there a few years—then moved to Gettysburg for a short time. He lives on a farm near Deckers Point at the present time.

Dr. Orlando C. Stewart, a native of Greenville, was educated at Greenville and Armagh Select Schools; studied medicine with Dr. Robert J. Tomb; graduated at the University of Maryland at Baltimore; located in Cookport in 1877, and practiced his profession there until 1889, when he moved to Bradford, Pa.

Dr. Herman L. McCullough, a native of Montgomery township, Indiana county, Pa., was educated at a select school at Cookport, Purchase Line and Greenville Academies and Indiana Normal School; studied medicine with Dr. H. B. Pitman; graduated at the Western Reserve Medical College, Cleveland, Ohio, in 1883; located in Cookport the same year and continues to pactice there until the present time.

Covode was laid out in 1840.

Dr. David M. Marshall, a native of Conemaugh township, Indiana county, Pa., was educated at the Jacksonville Academy; studied medicine with Dr. Thos. Mabon; graduated at the Jefferson Medical College, Philadelphia; located in Covode in 1850, and practiced his profession there until 1853, he then moved to Congruity, Westmoreland county, Pa, in a short time he moved to Salem in the same county, then to Ohio, (Jasper county.) In 1860 he moved to Homer City, Indiana county, Pa., and in 1864 to Marion Centre, and practiced there until 1872, then moved to Pittsburgh, had an office on Penn street for a few years; then moved to Homewood and afterwards to Brushton where he died. Dr. Marshall was Assistant Surgeon of 177th Regiment Pa. Vol. for 9 months and represented Indiana county in the Legislature in 1868-69.

Dr. J. Milton Shields moved from Smithport to Covode in 1867, and practiced there, except a few months in Indiana until 1877, then moved to New Mexico. (See Smithport.)

Dr. Winfield S. Shields practiced his profession in Covode during 1877, then returned to Marion. (See Marion.)

Dr. Joseph C. Golden moved from Armstrong county, Pa., to Covode about 1880, and died there a few years ago. (See Strongstown.)

Dr. J. Scheffer, a German physician, a graduate of the Hereford school of Science in Germany in 1865. When he came to the United States he located in Venango county, Pa., and practiced there until 1884, then moved to Covode and practiced there a few years, and moved to Allegheny county.

Diamondville first house built in 1824.

Dr. James D. Baldwin practiced in Diamondville and vicinity from 1846 to 1851, then moved to Allegheny City. He was the first settled physician in the village. (See Marion.)

Dr. A. Stansberry McClure, an Eclectic physician from Maine; located in Diamondville in 1851, and practiced there until 1862, then moved to Duncannon, Dauphin county, Pa., and is in Harrisburg at present.

Dr. Ambrose H. Myers, a native of Green township, was educated at select schools; studied medicine with Dr. Lovelace; graduated at the University of Maryland at Baltimore in 1882; located in Rue City, McKean county, Pa., and practiced there a short time, and moved to Diamondville, was there about a year, then moved to Mechaniesburg and remained there until 1887, then moved to Mount Pleasant, Westmoreland county, Pa., where he resides at present.

DIXONVILLE was laid out in 1860.

Dr. John J. Buchanan, a native of Westmoreland county, Pa., was educated at Twolick and Taylorsville select schools; studied medicine in Westmoreland county; attended lectures at Ann Arbor, Michigan; located in Dixonville, in 1868, and practice medicine there until his death in 1875.

Dr. John B. Green, a native of Cherryhill township, was raised in Altoona, Blair county, where he was educated; studied medicine with Dr. Sloan, at Chest Springs, Cambria county, Pa.; graduated at the Cincinnati College of Medicine and Surgery, Ohio, in 1876. He located in Dixonville in 1877, and practiced there until 1883, then he moved to Carrolltown, Cambria county, and remained there about two years, then moved to Summerhill in the same county where he resides at present.

Dr. James C. Short, moved from Marion to Dixonville in 1883 and practiced his profession there until 1886, then moved to his farm five miles east of Indiana. (See Marion.)

Dr. John C. McMillen, a native of Rayne township, was educated at the Marion Institute; studied medicine with Dr. Parke; graduated at the Western Reserve Medical College, Cleveland, Ohio, in 1884; located in Dixonville the same year, and has continued to practice his profession there to the present time.

Dr. A. Bryan Krebs, a native of Indiana county, was educated at the common schools, Marion Institute and the Ebensburg High school; studied medicine with Dr. D. S. Rice; graduated at the Cincinnati College of Medicine and Surgery in 1886; located in Dixonville the same year, practiced there seven months, then moved to Gettysburg and remained there two years, then moved to Lilly Station, Cambria county, Pa., where he resides at present.

GLENN CAMPBELL.

Dr. George M. Glasgow, located at Glenn Campbell in the summer of 1891. He graduated at the University of Maryland at Baltimore in 1890, and at the Jefferson Medical College, Philadelphia, in 1891.

GEORGEVILLE was laid out about 1830.

Dr. Robert K. Scott moved from Armagh to the vicinity of Georgeville in 1824, and practiced there a few years, then moved to Mercer county, Pa. (See Armagh.)

Dr. William Powell, an eastern physician, located in the neighborhood of Georgeville, shortly after Dr. Scott moved away and practiced there until 1834; then moved to Butler county, Pa.

Dr. P. P. Rich, a native of Connecticut, received his education in his native State. He was past the meridian of life when he came to Indiana county; he located in the vicinity of Georgeville about 1828, and lived on different farms. He was poor and had to labor under many disadvantages, but is represented as being a fine scholar and was highly appreciated as a physician. He moved to Ohio in 1836 and kept moving westward until his death. He is buried on the banks of the Mississippi river, three miles above Alton in Illinois.

Dr. Samuel McKee was raised at McKee's Mills, four miles north of Indiana, was educated at the Indiana Academy;

studied medicine with Dr. Rich; settled on a farm near Georgeville to practice his profession; he was in delicate health all his life and died in 1836.

Dr. *Thomas M. Laney*, a native of Maryland, where he was educated; studied medicine with Dr. Goodhart, of Dayton; graduated at the Medical Department of the University of Maryland at Baltimore; located in Georgeville in 1851; practiced there until 1853, then moved to Blairsville and practiced there until 1865, when he moved to Savannah, Missouri, and practiced there until his death, January 14th, 1891.

Dr. *William L. Morrow*, a native of Virginia, was educated at the Jacksonville Academy; studied medicine with Dr. Mahon graduated at the Jefferson Medical College, Philadelphia; located in Georgeville in 1853, and practiced his profession there until 1855, then moved to Elderton, Armstrong county, Pa., and practiced there a few years, then moved to Freeport in the same county, where he is at present.

Dr. *John S. McNutt*, a native of Brushvalley township, was educated at the common schools; studied medicine with Dr. Cresswell, of New Bethlehem, Clarion county, Pa.: graduated at the Cincinnati College of Medicine and Surgery; located in Georgeville in 1860, and practiced there until 1864, then moved to Clarksburg and remained there a short time, then moved to Apollo, then to Beaver, Pa. In 1872 he moved to Philadelphia where he resides at present.

Dr. *James Morrow*, a native of South Mahoning township, was educated at the Dayton Academy; studied medicine with Dr. C. McEwen; graduated at the Western Reserve Medical College, Cleveland, Ohio in 1867; located in Georgeville the same year and practiced his profession there eighteen months; then moved to Philadelphia and lived there one year, then moved to Sheakleyville, Mercer county, Pa.

Dr. *James R. Ewing*, a native of Conemaugh township, was educated at the Jacksonville Academy; studied medicine with Dr. Jack: graduated at the Medical College of Ohio, Cincinnati; located in Georgeville in 1872, and practiced there one year, and moved to Plumville and spent a year there, then moved to Louisville and remained a short time, then moved to Oakland Cross Roads, Westmoreland county, Pa., and practiced four years, then moved to Salem, in the same county, where he resides at present.

Dr. Edward H. Dickie, a native of West Wheatfield township, was educated at the common schools, Blairsville school and Normal School, Indiana, Pa.; studied medicine with Dr. Thomas St. Clair; graduated at the Medical Department of the University of Wooster, Cleveland, Ohio; located at Georgeville in 1884, practiced there two years, then moved to Kellysburg and remained there three months, then moved to Strongstown and remained there until July, 1891, then moved to Greenville where he is at present.

GETTYSBURG was laid out in 1851.

Dr. Joseph H. Ake, a native of Williamsburg, Blair county, Pa., was educated at Jefferson College, Cannonsburg, Pa.; studied medicine with Dr. J. D. Ross; graduated at Jefferson Medical College, Philadelphia; located in the vicinity of Gettysburg in 1850, and practiced there three years, then moved to Cherrytree and practiced there until 1855, and returned to Williamsburg, his native place and practiced there until his death, January 25, 1887.

Dr. John W. Crooks, a practitioner, came from York county, Pa., to Gettysburg in 1857, and practiced his profession there about three years, and then returned to his former home.

Dr. H. B. Pitman, a native of Green township, was educated at the common schools and select schools at Cherrytree and Mechanicsburg; studied medicine with Dr. W. A. Piatt; graduated at Ann Arbor, Michigan; located at Gettysburg in 1867, and continues to practice his profession in the same place to the present time.

Dr. A. Bryan Krebs moved from Dixonville to Gettysburg

in 1887, and practiced there about two years, and moved to Lilly Station, Cambria county, Pa., where he resides at present. (See Dixonville.)

Dr. J. Sloan Miller is a native of Grant township, was educated at the common schools, Marion Institute, select school at Homer City and Normal School, Indiana, Pa.; studied medicine with Dr. J. G. Campbell; graduated at the Baltimore Medical College in 1890; located in Gettysburg the same year and continues to practice his profession there.

GREENVILLE was laid out in 1839.

Dr. George Cleis, a Frenchman, who had been a surgeon in the Army in his native country, came to the United States, and located at Williamsport, Pa., remained there a short time, came to Greenville in 1841 and practiced his profession there about eighteen months, then moved to East Liberty, Allegheny county, Pa., practiced there a few years, when he was thrown from his sulkey and died the next day. He was the first settled physician in Greenville.

Dr. Wallace B. Stewart, a native of Philadelphia, where he received his prepartary education, lived a short time in Huntingdon county, Pa.; studied medicine with Dr. W. G. Stewart in Armagh; graduated at the Franklin Medical College. Philadelphia; located in Greenville in 1845 and practiced there until the fall of 1855, then moved to Indiana and entered into partnership in practice with Dr. Thomas St. Clair and in the spring of 1856 they dissolved partnership and Dr. Stewart returned to Greenville and resumed his business there. In the summer of 1885 he spent in Nebraska, and in 1859 he moved to Armagh and practiced his profession there until his death in 1875.

Dr. Thomas McMullen moved to Greenville in 1858 and practiced his profession there until his death, Feb. 12, 1884. (See Bell's Mills.)

Dr. Cicero M. Ewing moved from Strongstown to Greenville

in 1870 and practiced there about three years. (See Strongstown.)

Dr. J. McCune, a native of McKeesport, Allegheny county, Pa., was engaged in the Drugs business a short time; studied medicine with Dr. Thomas St.Clair; located in Greenville in 1855 and in 1856 moved to New Washington, Clearfield county, Pa., and practiced there several years, then moved to Old Virginia and engaged in the lumber business.

Dr. Hartwell, a native of Massachusetts, where he was educated and practiced a few years in Johnstown, Pa., moved to Greenville and practiced medicine there six months, and returned to Johnstown, and in a short time moved east.

Dr. Marshall, a physician from Lowell, Massachusetts, came to Greenville and entered into partnership with Dr. Hartwell; after a few months the Court of Quarter Sessions of the county transferred him to Allegheny City.

Dr. John M. Hadden, a native of Cherryhill township, Indiana county, Pa., was educated at the common schools and select schools at Plumville, Shelocta and Greenville; studied medicine with Dr. Thomas McMullen; attended lectures at Ann Arbor, Michigan; located in Greenville in 1870 and practiced there until August, 1872, then moved to Seymour, Champaigne county, Illinois, where he resides at present.

Dr. John W. Smith, a native of Green township, was educated at the common schools, Pine Flat and Cherrytree Academies and Reidsburg Institute, Clarion county, Pa.; studied medicine with Dr. Brallier; attended lectures, and practiced medicine several years in Greenville, then moved to Farmington, West Virginia, and practiced there several years, then moved to Clarksburg in the same State.

Dr. J. C. Wakefield, a native of West Wheatfield township, Indiana county, Pa., was educated at select schools; studied medicine with Dr. B. F. Tomb; graduated at the Western Reserve Medical College, Cleveland, Ohio, in 1878; located in

Greenville the same year and practiced his profession there about a year, then moved to Strongstown, and remained there about a year, then moved to Vinco, Cambria county, Pa., where he resides at present.

Dr. Norris Cameron, was born in Green township, Indiana county, Pa., March 20, 1856, was educated at the common schools, Purchase Line Academy and Cherrytree Male and Female College; studied medicine with Dr. Thomas McMullen; graduated at the Jefferson Medical College, Philadelphia, in 1880; located in Greenville the same year and practiced his profession there until 1888; then moved to Cherrytree and practiced there until February, 1891; then moved to Walls Station, Allegheny county, Pa., where he resides at present. Dr. Cameron attended partial course of lectures at the Bellevue Hospital College, University of New York and Poloclinic of New York. He is a member of the Indiana County Medical Society.

Dr. Thomas J. Henry was born in Apollo, Armstrong county, Pa., November 3, 1858; was educated at the public schools and select school in Apollo and at Eldersridge Academy; studied medicine with Dr. W. B. Ansley; graduated at the Medical Department of the University of Wooster, Cleveland, Ohio; located in Greenville in 1884, and practiced his profession there three years; then moved to Apollo, his native place, where he resides at present. Dr. Henry was a member of the Indiana County Medical Society when he was living in the county.

Dr. David P. Jackson was born near New Castle, Lawrence county, Pa., January 18, 1851; was educated at Westminister College, receiving the degree of Batchelor of Sciencee; studied medicine with Dr. John W. Wallace, of New Castle; graduated at the Miami Medical College, Cincinnat, Ohio, in 1874; located in New Castle the same year and practiced his profession there until 1883. He was city physician for New Castle and Coroner of Lawrence county for eight years; then moved to Lebanon, New Jersey in 1883; and practiced there until 1888; moved to Greenville, Indiana county, Pa., and in June, 1888 moved to

Blacklick Station and practiced his profession there until July, 1891; then moved to New Bedford, Lawrence county, Pa. Dr. Jackson was a member of the Indiana County Medical Society.

Dr. James Irwin Mabon, a native of East Mahoning township, Indiana county, Pa., was educated at the common school and Marion Institute; studied medicine with Dr. McEwen; graduated at the Western Pennsylvania Medical College, Pittsburgh, Pa., in 1888; located in Greenville the same year and continued to practice his profession there.

Dr. Edward H. Dickie moved from Strongstown to Greenville, July 1st, 1891, to practice his profession. (See Georgeville.)

HOMER CITY was laid out in 1834.

Dr. James Shields a native of Bairdstown, near Blairsville, was was the first physician in this place; was educated at the Blairsville schools; studied medicine with Dr. Marshall; attended a course of lectures at the Jefferson Medical College; spent a short time at New Florence, then moved to Lockport; located in Homer City in 1858 and practiced there about 18 months; then moved to West Lebanon; then to Westmoreland county, Pa.; then moved to Venango county, and finally to Cambria county where he died.

Dr. David M. Marshall moved from Jasper county, Ohio, to Homer City in 1860, and practiced his profession there until 1864, then moved to Marion. (See Covode.)

Dr. John Evans, a native of Brushvalley township, Indiana county, Pa., was born May 20, 1835; educated at the Mechanicsburg schools, Jacksonville and Saltsburg Academies; studied medicine with Dr. James McMullen; attended a course of lectures and located at Greenville in 1864 and ot Homer City in 1865, where he has been engaged in the practice of his profession to the present time. Dr. Evans served as Hospital Stewart during the late war.

Dr. John C. Morrison, a native of Westmoreland county, Pa., graduated at Jefferson College, Cannonsburg, Pa.; studied medicine in Latrobe; attended lectures at Jefferson Medical College,

HOMER CITY.

Philadelphia; located in Homer City in 1865 and practiced there until 1867, then moved to Taylorsville and practiced there about two years and then moved to Irwin, Westmoreland county.

Dr. D Burrell moved from Taylorsville to Homer City in 1867; practiced there two years; then moved to Westmoreland county. (See Taylorsville.)

Dr. Shadrach H. Thomas, a native of Clarion county; was educated at Reedsburg Institute, Clarion county; studied medicine with Dr. Thomas of Freeport; attended lectures and located in Homer City in 1873; practiced his profession there until 1876; then moved to the Pine Flat, remaining there about a year; then went to Texas; then returned to Reedsburg, Clarion county, Pa., remaining there a few years, from which place he moved to Maryland.

Dr. George F. Acuey, a native of Centre county, where he was educated and studied medicine; graduated at Jefferson Medical College; located in Homer City in 1878 and practiced his profession there one year; then moved to Altoona, Blair county, Pa., where he resides at present.

Dr. John A. Davis moved from Jacksonville to Homer City in 1881 and practiced there until 1884. (See Jacksonville.)

Dr. J. Gilbert Campbell was born near Armagh, East Wheatfield township, Indiana county, Pa., May 1, 1852; was educated at the public schools, Indiana and Eldersridge academies; studied medicine with Dr. R. J. Tomb; graduated at the college of Physicians and Surgeons of Baltimore, Md., in 1879; located at New Washington and practiced there until 1885; then moved to Homer City and has been engaged in professional work to the present time, in that place.

Dr. William L. Reed moved from Jacksonville to Homer City in 1889 and is engaged in practice there at present. (See Shelocta.

INDIANA was laid out in 1805.

Dr. Jonathan French, the first settled physician in Indiana, was a native of New Hampshire and received his education, literary and medical, in Vermont. He located in York, Pa., and and after practicing his profession there for some time, moved to Kittanning, Pa.; and in a short time to Indiana. He located in Indiana in 1807 and practiced there until his death, August 20, 1814. He is represented as being a man of fine culture and a successful physician. Dr. French was married to a daughter of Gen. Charles Campbell of Blacklick; Mrs. French died in 1818 and is buried beside her husband in the old grave yard on the south side of Indiana borough.

Dr. Robert Mitchell, a native of Ohio county, West Virginia, was educated at the best schools in the county at that time; he studied medicine with Dr. Mageehan, a prominent physician residing about 16 miles from Wheeling, West Virginia, at that time; attended a course of lectures at the University of Pennsylvania; located in Indiana in 1811 and soon entered on an extensive and lucrative practice which lasted for a number of years. He was partial to the so-called Rush system of treating disease and was very successful in certain forms of inflammatory affections. Dr. Mitchell represented Indiana county in the Legislature for five years. He was elected first in 1819 and was one of the associate judges of the county for five years, from 1836 to 1841. He had invested largely in real estate and for twenty years before his death had retired from active practice in his profession. He died April 14, 1863, aged 76 years.

Dr. James M. Stewart, a native of Huntingdon county, Pa., was educated at the best schools in his native county; studied medicine with Dr. Henderson of Huntingdon; graduated at the University of Pennsylvania; located in Indiana in 1814; in one year he returned to Huntingdon county; and at the end of the next year he returned to Indiana and continued to practice medicine and surgery until a short time before his death, March 27, 1869. Dr. Stewart was frequently called in consultation to Armstrong, Clarion, Clearfield, Jefferson and Westmoreland counties in difficult cases. Dr. Stewart represented Indiana county in the Legislature in 1831 and was appointed Associate Judge in 1849 for a term of three years.

Dr. Thomas Moorhead was born about two miles west of Indiana; was educated at the common schools and Indiana academy; studied medicine with Dr. Stewart; he was associated with Dr. Mitchell in practice in 1832 and 1833, but afterwards spent the greater part of his time in traveling through the thinly settled portions of Indiana and Clearfield counties. He died in the vicinity of Strongstown about 1834 or 1835.

Dr. George W. Gettys a native of Huntingdon county, Pa., where he was educated. In early life he was a printer; then studied medicine, and moved to Indiana and was associated in professional work for three years, with Dr. Mitchell; he moved to Armagh and practiced there one year; returned to Indiana and practiced a short time; then moved to Butler, Pa., to practice his profession, but in a short time bought the *Butler Whig* and published that paper for several years; then moved to Blairsville and published the *Blairsville Journal* for a few months; then moved back to his native county, and died a few years later.

Dr. Joseph Crooks a practitioner from Greencastle, Franklin county, Pa.; located in Indiana in 1840 and practiced there about three years, then moved to Ohio.

Dr. James M. Taylor a native of Indiana was educated at the Indiana and Harrisburg academies; taught school in Saltsburg, Pa., and Steubenville, Ohio; studied medicine with Dr. Stewart; graduated at Jefferson Medical College, Philadelphia; located in Indiana in 1843 and continued to practice medicine there until 1857; then moved to Kittanning, Pa., and remained there sixteen years; then returned to Indiana, where he resides at present.

Dr. Thomas St. Clair was born in White township, Indiana county, Pa; was educated at the public schools and Indiana academy; studied medicine with Dr. Jenks of Punxsutawney, Jefferson county, Pa., and completed his course of study with

Dr. James M. Stewart of Indiana; graduated at Jefferson Medical College, Philadelphia, in 1847; located the same year in Indiana and continued his professional work to this date in the same place, except a few months in East Liberty, Allegheny county, Pa. He represented Indiana and Armstrong counties in the State Senate during the years 1863 and 1864, and Indiana and Jefferson counties in the Senate from 1876 to 1880.

Dr. William Anderson, a native of Green township, Indiana county, Pa., was educated at the common schools and Blairsville and Indiana academies; studied medicine with Dr. J. M. Taylor; graduated at the Jefferson Medical College, Philadelphia; located in Indiana in 1851 and has continued in the practice of his profession in the same place to the present time. In the years 1868 and 1869 he returned to college and took a thorough Post graduate course. Dr. Anderson is a member of the Indiana County Medical Society; a permanent member of the Medical Society of the State of Pennsylvania since 1862; a permanent member of the American Medical Association since 1868; a member of the International Medical Congress and a member of the Inter-Continental American Medical Congress.

Dr. Hufeland, a German physician, located in Indiana in 1852 and remained about six months; then moved to the eastern part of the State.

Dr. William Altman moved from Punxsutawney to Indiana in 1853 and practiced nearly a year with Dr. St.Clair; then returned to Punxsutawney. (See Armagh.)

Dr. Samuel M. Swan a native of Armagh; was educated at the common schools and Washington College; studied medicine with Dr. Samuel F. Stewart; graduated at the Jefferson Medical College, Philadelphia; located in Indiana in 1854, was in partnership with Dr. St.Clair for a year; then moved to Illinois and spent a few years there; then returned to Johnstown, Pa., where he is engaged in practice to the present time.

Dr. Wallace B. Stewart moved from Greenville to Indiana in the fall of 1855 and practiced with Dr. St.Clair until 1859; then returned to Greenville. (See Greenville.)

Dr. William Reed moved from Beaver county, Pa., to Indiana in 1856, and practiced with Dr. St.Clair until 1856; then moved to Iberia, Ohio. (See Smicksburg.)

Dr. James S. McCartney a native of Armstrong county, Pa.; was educated at the Indiana academy and Jefferson College, Cannonsburg, Pa.; studied medicine; graduated at Jefferson Medical College, Philadelphia; located in Indiana in 1856 and practiced there about a year; then moved to Tarentum, Allegheny county, Pa., where he resides at present.

Dr. Robert Burr moved from Armagh to Indiana in 1859, and remained there until his death, March 2, 1882. (See Armagh.)

Dr. James T. Adair, a native of Indiana county, Pa.; was educated at the common schools and Jacksonville academy; studied medicine with Dr. Mabon; graduated at the Jefferson Medical College, Philadelphia, in 1860; located in Indiana the same year; moved to Cherrytree about the end of the same year. In the fall of 1861 he moved to Mt.Jackson, Lawrence county, Pa., and practiced there until 1863 he was appointed assistant surgeon of the 77th regiment, Pa. Vol. Infantry; in 1865 his health failed and he returned to his parents' home near Greenville and died May 5, 1866, from consumption.

Dr. John K. Thompson moved from Marion to Indiana in 1863 and practiced with Dr. St.Clair until 1865; then returned to Marion. (See Marion.)

Dr. Herman Row a native of Greensburg, Pa.; spent his early life in Somerset; was educated at the Indiana academy; studied medicine with Dr. McCormick of Grantsville, Md.; graduated at the University of Pennsylvania; located in Indiana in 1865 and practiced there until 1873; then moved to Altoona, Blair county, Pa., and remained there until his death, in 1879.

Dr. Augustus F. Purington a native of Maine; was educated at the Maine Wesleyan Seminary; studied medicine with Dr.

James McKeene of Topsham, Maine; attended a course of lectures at the Medical Department of Dartmoth College, New Hampshire; graduated at the Bowdoin Medical College, Maine, in 1864; served acting assistant surgeon about fourteen months; located in Indiana in 1866, and has continued to practice his profession here to the present time. For several years after he settled in Indiana he was in partnership with Dr. St.Clair, then they dissolved. Dr. Purington is a member of the Indiana County Medical Society, and a member of the Medical Society of the State of Pennsylvania.

Dr. James M. Torrence was born in Punxsutawney, Jefferson county, Pa., December 6, 1845. He spent two years and a half learning the printing business in Indiana; after the war he attended the Iron City Business College, then the Glade Run Academy and Mount Union College; studied medicine with Dr. John W. Hughes in Blairsville; graduated at the Jefferson Medical College, Philadelphia, in 1873; located in Indiana and has continued to practice his profession in the same place. Dr. Torrence was a soldier in the late rebellion; he enlisted, before he was sixteen years of age, in company K., 105th regiment, Pa. Volunteers.

Dr. William N. Cunningham moved from Jacksonville to Indiana in the fall of 1877, and remained there about two years; he then returned to Jacksonville, where he lives at present. (See Jacksonville.)

Dr. Charles M. St.Clair a native of Indiana, Pa., was educated at the Indiana schools; studied medicine with his father, Dr. Thomas St.Clair; graduated at the Jefferson Medical College, Philadelphia, in 1878, and practiced medicine with his father in Indiana until 1887; then moved to Latrobe, Westmoreland county, Pa., and retired from the practice of medicine.

Dr. N. Frank Ehrenfeld a native of Armstrong county, Pa.; part of his early life was spent in Johnstown, Pa.; was educated at the Indiana High school and State Normal school at

California, Pa.; studied medicine with Dr. Purington; graduated at the University of Pennsylvania in 1880; entered into partnership the same year with Dr. Barr in the practice of medicine; this partnership continued until the death of Dr. Barr in March 1882, and has continued in the practice of his profession in Indiana to the present time.

Dr. *Arthur Devoe* a native of New York State, where he was educated and studied medicine; graduated at the University of Buffalo, New York, in 1875; located at Meadville, Pa.; practiced there a short time, and moved to Indiana and practiced as a homœopathist for several years; then moved to Buffalo, New York; then to Blairsville, and in a short time to Seattle, Washington, where he registered as a regular physician.

Dr. *Marmora Devoe* a graduate of the Homeopathic Medical College of Cleveland, Ohio, in 1877. She moved from Steubenville, Ohio to Indiana in 1881, and practiced her system here for a year; then returned to Steubenville, Ohio. She is now at Seattle, State of Washington.

Dr. *George Hunter* moved from Blairsville to Indiana in 1886; practiced there a few months; then returned to Blairsville. (See Blairsville.)

Dr. *David B. Sturgeon* a native of Armstrong county, Pa., where he was educated; studied medicine with Dr. Thomas H. Allison in Elderton; graduated at Columbia Medical College, D. C., in 1860; located in Uniontown, Pa., where he practiced his profession a short time; then moved to Ohio; then to New York State; then moved to Indiana in 1882, and practiced part of a year; then moved to Pittsburgh, Pa.

Dr. *William Hosack* moved from West Lebanon to Indiana in the fall of 1887, and resides there at the present time. (See West Lebanon.)

Dr. *John M. St. Clair* was born about two miles southwest of Indiana; was educated at the Indiana High school and LaFayette College, Easton, Pa.; studied medicine with Drs. St.

Clair and Purington; graduated at the University of Pennsylvania in 1875; located at Elderton, Armstrong county, Pa., the same year and practiced his profession there until April, 1890; then moved to Indiana, where he resides at present. Dr. St. Clair is a member of the Indiana County Medical Society.

JACKSONVILLE was laid out in 1830.

Dr. Augustus H. Gross was the first physician in Jacksonville; he came from Pittsburgh, Pa., in 1840, and practiced medicine in Jacksonville and vicinity for eight years; then moved to East Liberty, Allegheny county, Pa., where he continued to practice medicine until his death in 1877.

Dr. Thomas Mabon a native of Mahoning township, Indiana county, Pa.; was educated at the common and select schools of the county; studied medicine with Dr. Liggett, of Centreville; attended a course of lectures at Glasgow, Scotland; graduated at the Jefferson Medical College, Philadelphia; located in Jacksonville in 1848 and practiced his profession there for fifteen years; he moved to Allegheny City in 1863, and practiced there until his death, November 23, 1890. Dr. Mabon was a member of the Indiana County Medical Society while he lived in the county.

Dr. George Irvin moved from Plumville to Jacksonville in 1858, and practiced there two years. (See Plumville.)

Dr. Joseph F. Stewart moved from Taylorsville to Jacksonville in 1864 and practiced there until his death, September 21, 1865. (See Taylorsville.)

Dr. William Jack was born two miles south of Jacksonville; was educated at the common schools, Eldersridge Academy, and graduated at Washington College, Washington, Pa.; studied medicine with Dr. Mabon; graduated at the Jefferson Medical College, Philadelphia; was appointed assistant surgeon to the 177th regiment, Pa. Vols., and served in that position nine months; was then appointed surgeon to 84th regiment, P. V., and served to the close of the war; then located in Jacksonville and practiced his profession there nine years. In 1874 he moved to Allegheny City, where he resides at present. Dr. Jack was a member of the Indiana County Medical Society while living in the county.

Dr. *Samuel M. Elder* was born two miles east of Armagh; was educated at the Indiana and Saltsburg Academies; studied medicine with Dr. Barr; graduated at the Jefferson Medical College, Philadelphia; shortly after he graduated, he entered the army and served for three years. At the close of the war he located in Jacksonville and practiced medicine there until his health failed and he was compelled to abandon his profession, and returned to the home of his parents, near Armagh, where he died June 17, 1868.

Dr. *William C. Parker*, a native of Ohio, near Columbus; was educated and studied medicine in Columbus; graduated at the Starling Medical College, Columbus, Ohio; located in Jacksonville in 1869 and practiced there about a year; then moved to Mansfield, Allegheny county, Pa., and practiced there a few years; then moved to Los Angeles, California.

Dr. *Christopher C. Miller*, a native of Brushvalley township, Indiana county, Pa.; was educated at the Mechanicsburg Academy and Mt. Union College, Ohio; studied medicine with Dr. B. F. Tomb; graduated at the Medical College of Ohio at Cincinnati; located at Belsano, Cambria county, Pa., in 1869, and moved to Jacksonville in 1870; practiced his profession there until 1876; then moved to Gallitzin, Cambria county, Pa., and practiced there a few years then moved to Henry county, Illinois.

Dr. *William N. Cunningham*, a native of Young township, Indiana county, Pa., was educated at Eldersridge Academy; studied medicine with Dr. Jack; graduated at the Jefferson Medical College, Philadelphia; located in Jacksonville in 1864 and practiced there until the fall of 1877; he moved to Indiana and remained there over a year, then returned to Jacksonville, where he resides at present.

Dr. *William L. Reed* moved from Shelocta to Jacksonville

in 1875 and practiced his profession there until 1889, when he moved to Homer City, where he resides at present. (See Shelocta.)

Dr. *John A. Davis*, a native of Armstrong township, Indiana county, Pa.; was educated at the common schools and Elderton Academy; studied medicine with Dr. Thomas St.Clair; graduated at Ann Arbor Medical College, Michigan; located at Leland, Illinois, and practiced there five years; then moved to Jacksonville in 1878 and practiced there a short time; moved to Homer City and practiced a few years; then returned to Leland, Illinois, where he resides at present.

Dr. *James G. Davis* a native of Armstrong township, Indiana county, Pa.; was educated at the common schools and Jacksonville Academy; studied medicine with Dr. John A. Davis; graduated at the Jefferson Medical College, Philadelphia; located in Jacksonville in 1880 and practiced his profession there until the fall of 1886; he then visited California for his health, and returned to Jacksonville in 1887, but did not undertake active practice; he died June, 1888.

Dr. *William Lincoln Shields* a native of Plumville; was educated at the Plumville Select school and Dayton Academy; studied medicine with Dr. C. McEwen; graduated at the medical department of the University of Louisville, Kentucky, in 1885; located at Dayton, Armstrong county, Pa.; practiced there a short time; then moved to Girty in the same county; practiced there until early in the year 1889; he then moved to Jacksonville, where he resides at present. Dr. Shields is a member of the Indiana County Medical Society.

KIMMEL.

Dr. *George Martin*, a native of Kimmel; was educated at the common schools and Greenville Academy; studied medicine with Dr. Thomas McMullen; graduated at the Jefferson Medical College, Philadelphia; located at Kimmel in 1885 and practiced his profession there until the fall of 1886; then moved to Cherrytree and practiced his profession there until 1888; then returned to Kimmel and remained there until April 1, 1890; he moved to Johnstown, Cambria county, Pa. Dr. Martin is the only physician who lived and practiced at Kimmel.

WEST LEBANON was laid out in 1839.

Dr. William Craig was born near the town of Marion. He learned a trade and after working at it for some time attended Select schools and studied medicine at Apollo; located in West Lebanon about 1840 but did not remain there long. He moved to Jenner Cross Roads, Somerset county, Pa., and practiced there a few years; then moved to Wheeling, West Virginia, and practiced there a few years; then graduated at the Western Reserve Medical College, Cleveland, Ohio; in 1852 he moved to Keosauqua, Van Buren county, Iowa, where he practiced his profession to the present time.

Dr. Hugh Adair was born three miles south of Indiana; was educated at the common schools and Indiana Academy; studied medicine with Dr. Jackson in Blairsville; graduated at the Franklin Medical College, Philadelphia; located in West Lebanon in 1847 and practiced there a few years; then moved to Emlenton, Venango county, and a few years later to Anandale, Butler county, Pa., where he died.

Dr. James D. McClure a native of Westmoreland county, Pa.; was educated and studied medicine in his native county; graduated at the Jefferson Medical College, Philadelphia; located in West Lebanon in 1851 and practiced his profession there for two years; in 1853 he moved to Armagh, and in the fall of 1854 to one of the western States.

Dr. J. C. Edgar, a native of Westmoreland county, Pa.; where he was educated; studied medicine in Livermore and practiced there for some time; then moved to West Lebanon in 1853 and practiced there until 1857, when he retired from practice.

Dr. George R. Lewis, a native of Indiana county, Pa.; was educated at Eldersridge Academy and Washington College, Washington, Pa.; studied medicine with Dr. D. R. Lewis, of

Ebensburg; graduated at the Jefferson Medical College, Philadelphia; located in Washington county in 1857, and in 1858 moved to West Lebanon and practiced there about six months; then moved to Ebensburg, Cambria county, Pa., and remained three years. He served as assistant surgeon and surgeon in the army the following three years. In 1865 he moved to Indiana and went into the drug and apothecary business and continued in the business until 1882, when he moved to St. Paul, Minnesota.

Dr. *James Shields* moved from Homer City to West Lebanon in 1859 and practiced there a short time. (See Homer City.)

Dr. *Samuel W. Virtue*, a native of Ireland; was raised in Centre township; was educated at the common schools and Jacksonville Academy; studied medicine with Dr. Mahon; graduated at the Charity Hospital College, Cleveland, Ohio; located at Maysville, Armstrong county, Pa., in 1865; practiced there until 1870, when he moved to West Lebanon and practiced his profession there until his death, in 1873.

Dr. *Palmer*, a native of Burrell township; studied medicine in Blairsville; located in West Lebanon in 1870; remained there a short time, then moved to Michigan.

Dr. *William Hosack*, a native of Blacklick township, Indiana county, Pa.; was a soldier during the late war. He was educated at the common schools and Glade Run Academy; taught school several terms; studied medicine with Dr. Banks; graduated at the Jefferson Medical College, Philadelphia; located in West Lebanon in 1871 and practiced his profession there until 1879; he moved to Cherrytree and practiced his profession there until 1882, when he left Cherrytree, and in 1883 located again in West Lebanon and practiced there until the fall of 1887; he then moved to Indiana, where he resides at present. Dr. Hosack is a member of the Indiana County Medical Society.

Dr. *William T. Larimer*, a native of Westmoreland county; was educated at the common schools, Saltsburg and Glade Run Academies; studied medicine with Dr. Crawford; graduated at the Jefferson Medical College, Philadelphia; located in West

Lebanon in 1879 and practiced his profession there until 1883; moved to Saltsburg and practiced his profession there until 1888; then moved to Allegheny City, where he resides at present.

Dr. John T. Cass, a native of New Hartford, Oneida county, New York; was educated in the public schools in Otsego county, New York, and West Winfield Academy; taught school several years in Waterloo, Seneca county, N. Y.; studied medicine with Dr. S. R. Wells, of Waterloo, N. Y.; graduated at the University of New York City, N. Y., in 1887; located in West Lebanon, Indiana county, Pa., the same year, and continues to practice his profession in that place to the present time. Dr. Cass is a member of the Indiana County Medical Society.

LOUISVILLE was laid out in 1840.

Dr. James M. Ewing moved from Plumville to Louisville in 1874; remained there a short time. (See Georgeville.)

Dr. Benjamin C. Irwin moved from Shelocta to Louisville in 1890; remained there a short time. (See Shelocta.)

MARCHAND was laid out in 1860.

Dr. J. J. J. Bishop, a practitioner from Brookville, Jefferson county, Pa.; located in Marchand in 1859 and practiced his profession there eight years; moved to Punxsutawney, and in a short time returned to Brookville; a few years later he commenced the practice of dentistry. He was the first physician at Marchand.

Dr. Samuel C. Allison a native of Clarion county, Pa., where he was educated and studied medicine; graduated at the Jefferson Medical College, Philadelphia; located at Marchand in 1863 and practiced there about two years; then moved to Punxsutawney, where he resides at present.

Dr. James N. Loughry was born two miles south of Indiana borough; was educated at the common schools; studied medicine with Dr. Marshall; attended lectures at the Cincinnati College of Medicine and Surgery; located at Harrison City, Westmoreland county, Pa.; practiced there a few years; in

1865 he moved to Marchand, lived there a short time then moved to Marion, where he practiced his profession until 1872; moved to Penn Station, then to Pittsburgh, Pa.

Dr. *John B. Bair*, a native of Allegheny county, Pa., where he was educated and studied medicine; graduated at the Jefferson Medical College, Philadelphia; located at Marchand in 1867 and practiced his profession there until late in the fall of 1868; returned to Allegheny county, Pa., and died the latter part of the winter.

Dr. *A. H. Armstrong* was born near Shelocta; was educated at the Dayton and Elderton Academies; studied medicine with Dr. McChesney; attended a course of lectures at the Jefferson Medical College; located in Marchand in 1867 and moved to Pine Flat in 1869 and practiced there until his death, in 1874.

Dr. *John Wilson Morrow* was born in South Mahoning township, Indiana county, Pa., July 15, 1849; was educated at the common schools and Dayton Academy; studied medicine with Dr. C. McEwen; graduated at the Jefferson Medical College, Philadelphia; located at Marchand in 1873 and has been engaged in the practice of his profession in the same place to the present time. Dr. Morrow was elected to represent Indiana county in the Legislature of Pennsylvania in 1890.

MARION was laid out in 1842—now Marion Center.

Dr. *James D. Baldwin* was the first settled physician in Marion. He was a native of Boston, Massachusetts, where he was educated and studied medicine. When he came to Pennsylvania he located in Chester county, Pa., and practiced there a short time; then moved to Warrior's Mark, Huntingdon county, Pa., and practiced there several years; moved to Marion, Indiana county, Pa., in 1844 and practiced there about two years and a half; then moved to Diamondville; practiced medicine and was engaged in the lumber business in that place and vicinity until 1851; he then moved to Allegheny City and practed there until 1861; then moved to Oil City and spent the balance of his life in the oil business.

Dr. *John K. Thompson* was born in Stonerstown, Center county, Pa., December 25, 1821. He was educated at the common schools in his native place and at Allegheny College, Meadville, Pa.; studied medicine with Dr. George B. Engle, of Bellefont; attended a course of lectures at the Jefferson Medical College; located in Marion, Indiana county, Pa., March, 1846, and practiced his profession there until 1863; then moved to Indiana, Pa., and entered into partnership with Dr. Thomas St.Clair. At the end of two years they dissolved and Dr. Thompson returned to Marion and remained there until his death, September 17; 1890. Dr. Thompson was elected one of the Associate Judges of the county in 1856 and held the office ten years. In 1874 he was elected a member of the Legislature of Pennsylvania and re-elected in 1875. He was buried in Gilgal cemetery.

Dr. *John B Darison*, a native of Westmoreland county, Pa., where he was educated and studied medicine; graduated at the Jefferson Medical College, Philadelphia; located in Marion in 1851 and practiced his profession there until 1856; then moved to New Alexandria, Westmoreland county; remained there a short time and moved to Moline, Illinois where he resides at present.

Dr. *William Anthony* moved from Chambersville to Marion in 1856 and practiced his profession there until 1864, and moved to Kansas. (See Plumville.)

Dr. *George J. McHenry* moved from Taylorsville to Marion in 1864 and remained there until his death, July 10, 1891.

Dr. *David M. Marshall* moved from Homer City to Marion in 1865, and practiced his profession there until 1872, then moved Pittsburgh, Pa. (See Covode.)

Dr. *James N. Loughry* moved from Marchand to Marion in 1865 and lived there until 1871, then he moved to Westmoreland county. (See Marchand.)

Dr. *D. Harrold Snowden*, a native of Virginia; received a College education; studied medicine with Prof. Dunglison and graduated at the Jefferson Medical College; practiced medicine in Allegheny county, Pa., and located in Marion in 1873 and practiced there about two years; then retired from the practice of medicine; moved to Toledo, Ohio, and entered the ministry.

Dr. Winfield S. Shields, a native of Rayne township, Indiana county, Pa., was born Dec. 6, 1847; was educated at the common schools and Covode Academy; studied medicine with Dr. J. Milton Shields; graduated at Albany Medical College, N. Y.; located in Marion in 1874 and lived there until 1877; then moved to Covode and remained there a short time and returned to Marion, where he resides at present. Dr. Shields was a soldier during the late war.

Dr. A. H. Allison located in Marion in 1880 and continues to practice his profession there. (See Cookport.)

Dr. William E. Dodson moved from Newville to Marion in 1882 and is there at present. (See Smicksburg.)

Dr. James C. Short, a native of Huntingdon county, Pa.; was raised in Rayne township, Indiana county, Pa., was educated at the common schools; studied medicine with Dr. George J. McHenry; graduated at the Jefferson Medical College, Philadelphia; located in Marion in 1882 and practiced there until 1883 then moved to Dixonville and practiced there until 1886; then moved to a farm five miles east of Indiana where he continues his professional work. Dr. Short was a soldier during the late war, Co. A, 61st Reg't. Pa. Vol.

MECHANICSBURG was layed out in in 1833.

Dr. Hildebrand, a practioner in Somerset county, Pa., moved to Mechanicsburg in 1839 and remained there about six months; then returned to former home. He was the first settled physician in the place.

Dr. Livingston came to Mechanicsburg in 1840 and practiced medicine there fore eighteen months and left the place. No history.

Dr. Ferdinand F. Bengell came from Germany to Mechanicsburg in 1843 and practiced there about two your years; then

moved to Johnstown, Pa., and few years later moved to Marietta, Ohio, and in a short time returned to Johnstown and practiced his profession there until his death about 1865.

Dr. Henry Faulk, a practitioner from Germany, located in Mechanicsburg in 1845 and practiced there until 1849, then moved to Ohio.

Dr. James McMullen was born five miles southwest of Indiana, in Centre township, was educated at the common schools and Indiana Academy and Jefferson College, Canonsburg, Pa.; studied medicine with Dr. Augustus H. Gross; graduated at the Jefferson Medical College, Philadelphia; located in Mechanicsburg in 1849, and has been in the regular practice of his profession in the same place to the present time. Dr. McMullen is a member of the Indiana County Medical Society, and of the Medical Society of the State of Pennsylvania.

Dr. Thomas McMullen, practiced medicine in Mechanicsburg in 1854 and 1855. (See Blacklick.)

Dr. A. H. Myers moved from Diamondville to Mechanicsburg in 1882, and practiced there until 1887; then moved to Mount Pleasant, Westmoreland county. (See Diamondville.)

Dr. Benjamin F. Tomb moved from Armagh to Mechanicsburg in 1867, and practiced there until 1882; then moved to Morrellville, Cambria county, Pa., where he resides at present. (See Armagh.)

Dr. William J. George was born in Derry township, Westmoreland county, Pa., April 21, 1856; was educated at the common schools, Blairsville and Livermore Academies; studied medicine with Dr. Banks; graduated at the Medical Department of the University of Wooster, Cleveland, Ohio, in 1881; located in Fayette county, Pa., and practiced there until November, 1883; then moved to Mechanicsburg, Indiana county, Pa., and practiced there until the spring of 1886; then moved to Johnstown, Pa., where he resides at present; practicing his profession.

Dr. Joseph H. Smith, a native of Armstrong county, Pa., where he was educated, and studied medicine; graduated at the Western Reserve Medical College, Cleveland, Ohio; located at Apollo, Armstrong county, Pa., in 1876; practiced there until 1880, then moved to Dayton, in the same county, and in 1887 to Mechanicsburg and practiced there until the Spring of 1890. He concluded to visit the southwestern territories for the benefit of his health. He died at Guthrie, Oklahoma, August 15, 1890, aged 38 years.

Dr. G. W. Miller, a native of Brushvalley township, Indiana county, Pa. After he received his preparatory education; studied medicine with Dr. St.Clair; graduated at the Western Reserve Medical College, Cleveland, Ohio; located at Scalp Level, Cambria county, Pa., practiced there a short time; then moved to Gallitzin in the same county; and for the last three years has been practicing in the vicinity of Mechanicsburg.

NEWVILLE was laid out in 1854.

Dr. Theodore B. Gamble, a native of Susquehanna county, Pa., where he was educated; studied medicine with Dr. Horton, of Bradford county, Pa., attended lectures at Jefferson Medical College and Ann Arbor, Michigan; located in Newville in 1858; practiced there two years, then moved to a farm near Burlinggame, Kansas. He was the first settled physician in Newville.

Dr. Chalmers S. McCrea, was born in Saltsburg, Pa.; was educated at the Indiana Schools, Dayton and Mechanicsburg Academies; studied medicine with Dr. James McMullen; graduated at the Jefferson Medical College, Philadelphia, in 1875; located at Newville in the same year and practiced his profession there until 1881; then moved to New Bethlehem, Clarion county, Pa., and remained there about one year, and returned to Newville and practiced there until his death, January 27, 1887. Dr. McCrea was a soldier during the war and was a member of the Indiana County Medical Society.

Dr. Alonza Lowman, a native of Jacksonville, was educated

at Jacksonville High School and State Normal School, Indiana Pa.; studied medicine with Dr. Cunningham; graduated at the Jefferson Medical College, Philadelphia; located in Newville in 1881; practiced there a few months when his health failed, he returned to the home of his father at Jacksonville where he died in 1882.

Dr. William E. Dodson moved from Smicksburg to Newville in 1881; practiced there a few months then moved to Marion. (See Smicksburg.)

Dr. Harvey E. McAfoos, was born near Rural Village, Armstrong county, Pa., January 22, 1864; was educated at the Butler Orphan Home and Plumville Select School; studied medicine with Drs. McEwen; graduated at Western Pennsylvania Medical College, Pittsburgh, Pa., in 1887; located in Newville the same year and practiced there until 1890, when he removed to Latrobe, Westmoreland county, Pa., where he resides at present.

Dr. James A. Bryson, a native of Butler county, Pa., was born near Butler, April 12th, 1854; was educated at Edinborough Normal School, Erie county, Pa., and Westminster College; studied medicine with Dr. Zimmerman, of Butler, Pa; graduated at the Medical College of Ohio, Cincinnati, in 1880; located the same year at Worthington, Armstrong county, Pa., and practiced his profession there until 1890; when he moved to Newville, Indiana county, Pa., where he resides at present.

NOLO was laid out in 1845.

Dr. J. B. Luke, a native of Blair county, Pa., where he was educated; studied medicine with Dr. Smith, in Hollidaysburg, Pa., graduated at the Western Reserve Medical College, Cleveland, Ohio; located in Nolo in 1869 and practiced there two years; then moved to South Fork, Cambria county, Pa., where he resides at present. He is the only physician that settled in Nolo.

PINE FLAT was laid out in 1860.

Dr. J. A. Blose located at Pine Flat in April, 1880, and practiced his profession there until December, 1881; then moved to Cherrytree. (See Cherrytree.)

Dr. A. H. Armstrong moved from Marchand to Pine Flat in 1867 and practiced there until his death in 1874. He is buried at Shelocta and was the first settled physician at Pine Flat. (See Marchand.)

Dr. Shadrach H. Thomas moved from Homer City to Pine Flat in 1876, and remained there about a year. (See Homer City.)

Dr. Abram R. Lovelace moved from Cherrytree to Pine Flat in 1878 and practiced there two years, and in 1880 returned to Cherrytree. (See Cherrytree.)

Dr. John W. Dunwoodie, a native of Green township, was raised near Pine Flat, was educated at the common schools and Pine Flat Academy; studied medicine with Dr. Griffith, of Warrior's Mark, Huntingdon county, Pa.; graduated at the University of Pennsylvania in 1871; located at Glen Hope, Clearfield county, Pa., and practiced his profession there until 1883; then moved to Pine Flat and practiced there two years. In 1885 he moved to Phillipsburg, Centre county, Pa., where he resides at present.

Dr. C. B. Smith, a practitioner from Centre county, Pa., moved to Pine Flat in the fall of 1889, remained a few months and moved away.

PLUMVILLE was laid out in 1844.

Dr. John McAdoo, a native of Young township, Indiana county, Pa.; was educated at the common schools and Clearfield Academy; studied medicine with Dr. A. H. Gross; located in Plumville in 1844 and practiced there a short time; then moved West. He was the first settled physician in Plumville.

Dr. George Goodhart, a native of Huntingdon county, Pa.; where he was educated and studied medicine; located in Plumville in 1845 and practiced there two years; then moved to Dayton, Armstrong county, Pa., and practiced his profession there until his death in 1853.

PINE FLAT.

Dr. Samuel G. Berryhill, a native of Washington county, Pa.; where he was educated; studied medicine with Dr. Jackson, in Blairsville; graduated at the Jefferson Medical College; located in Plumville in 1849, where he remained in his professional work until his death in 1857.

Dr. William McEwen, a native of South Mahoning township, Indiana county, Pa.; was educated at the common schools, and Kittanning Academy; studied medicine with Dr. Goodhart; graduated at the Jefferson Medical College, Philadelphia, in 1852; located at Worthington, Armstrong county, Pa., and practiced there about a year; then moved to the vicinity of Plumville, and remained there until his death in 1855.

Dr. William Anthony, a native of Armstrong township, Indiana county, Pa.; was educated at the common schools, Eldersridge Academy and Jefferson College, Canonsburg, Pa.; studied medicine with Dr. Robert McChesney; graduated at the Jefferson Medical College, Philadelphia; located in Plumville, practiced there a short time; moved to Chambersville and in 1856 to Marion, and practiced his profession there until 1864, then moved to Alatha, Johnston county, Kansas; he lives at Prescott Station, Linn county, Kansas, at present. Dr. Anthony was a member of the Indiana County Medical Society while he resided in the county.

Dr. George Irvin, a native of Conemaugh township, Indiana county, Pa., was educated at the common schools and at the Jacksonville Academy; studied medicine with Dr. Mabon; graduated at Jefferson Medical College, Philadelphia; located in Prospect, Butler county, in 1855, and in 1856 moved to Plumville, Indiana county, and practiced there until 1858 then moved to Jacksonville and practiced there one year. In 1859 he moved to Aledo, Illinois, where he resides at present. Dr. Irvin was a member of the Indiana County Medical Society while he lived in the county.

Dr. Christopher McEwen was born in South Mahoning township, Indiana county, Pa., October 17, 1830; was raised on a farm; educated at the public schools in Plumville and Glade Run Academy; studied medicine with Dr. William McEwen; graduated at the Jefferson Medical College, Philadelphia, in 1855; located in Plumville the same year and has remained in regular practice in the same place to the present time.

Dr. Jones, a practitioner from Clarion county, Pa., moved to Plumville in 1858; remained there a few months and returned to Clarion county.

Dr. Joseph W. McEwen, a native of South Mahoning township, Indiana county, Pa., was educated at the public schools of Plumville, Dayton and Glade Run Academies; studied medicine with Dr. C. McEwen; graduated at the Jefferson Medical College, Philadelphia; located in Plumville in 1859 and practiced there about three years; then moved to Philadelphia, 1705 Christian street, and practiced there until 1869; he visited California and when he returned entered the navy and spent several years traveling in foreign countries; then settled again in Philadelphia, 402 South Broad street.

Dr. Joseph M. Ansley, a native of South Mahoning township, Indiana county; was educated at the public schools and Glade Run Academy; studied medicine with Dr. C. McEwen; attended lectures and located in Plumville in 1863, and practiced there until 1867, when he moved to Swedona, Mercer county, Illinois, where he resides at present.

Dr. William B. Ansley was born in South Mahoning township, Indiana county, August 2, 1847; he was educated at the common schools and Dayton Academy; taught school several terms; studied medicine a short time with Dr. C. McEwen; then entered the office of Dr. R. S. Sutton (at that time in Philadelphia) graduated at the Jefferson Medical College, Philadelphia, in 1867; located in Plumville the same year; practiced a short time there, then moved to Elderton, Armstrong county, Pa., and practiced there a short time; then moved to Apollo in the same county and practiced there until 1880, when he moved to Saltsburg where he resides at present. Dr. Ansley is a member of the Indiana County Medical Society and a member of the Medical Society of the State of Pennsylvania.

Dr. James M. Ewing moved from Georgeville to Plumville in 1873 and remained there one year, then moved to Louisville. (See Georgeville.)

Dr. Charles M. McEwen, a native of Plumville, was educated at the Plumville High School and Dayton Academy; studied medicine with his father, Dr. C. McEwen; graduated at Jefferson Medical College, Philadelphia, in 1879; entered into partnership with his father the same year in practice of medicine and has continued to practice in Plumville to the present time.

RICHMOND was laid out in 1862.

Dr. William E. Dodson moved from Marion to Richmond in 1884 and returned to Marion in 1887. (See Smicksburg.)

Dr. Samuel Albert Shaffer is a native of Plumcreek township, Armstrong county, Pa.; was born September 11, 1861; was educated at the common schools and Atwood Academy; studied medicine with Dr. C. A. Duff, of Atwood; graduated at the Western Pennsylvania Medical College, Pittsburgh, Pa., in 1889; located the same year in Richmond, Indiana county, Pa., where he is engaged in the practice of his profession.

SALTSBURG was laid out in 1827.

Before there was a settled physician in Saltsburg, Dr. Kirkpatrick, a Westmoreland county physician, practiced his profession around Saltsburg and several miles east of town. He resided about two miles west of Saltsburg. He was a very successful physician.

Dr. Benjamin Sterrett, a native of Cumberland valley; graduated at Dickinson College, Carlisle, Pa.; studied medicine there and located at Salem Cross Roads, Westmoreland county, Pa., in 1818; and practiced there until 1824; then moved to the prospective town of Saltsburg. At a later date he attended lectures at the Jefferson Medical College. He practiced in Saltsburg until 1836, then moved to Congruity, Westmoreland county, and practiced there until 1850; then returned to Saltsburg and practiced there until his death in 1865.

Dr. *John McFarland*, a native of Allegheny county, Pa., where he was educated; studied medicine with Dr. Charles Snowden, of Freeport, Pa.; graduated at the Jefferson Medical College, Philadelphia; practiced his profession a short time in Allegheny county and a few weeks at Salem, Westmoreland county. He located in Saltsburg in 1836 and practiced his profession there until his death, September 24th, 1889, with the exceptions of a few months in Monongahela City. Dr. McFarland represented Indiana county in the Legislature during the years 1844-45.

Dr. *Thomas Murray*, a native of the Susquehanna valley, was educated at the common schools and Milton Academy; studied medicine and graduated at the University of Pennsylvania; located in Saltsburg, Indiana county, Pa., in 1837, and soon obtained an extensive and lucrative practice and continued to practice for several years; then he retired in a general way from practice, dealing in real estate and farming in our county. About 1880 he moved to Beaver, Pa., where he resides at present.

Dr. *David R. Allison* was born six miles southwest of Indiana; was educated at the Indiana Academy; studied medicine with Dr. Mitchell; attended lectures at the University of Pennsylvania; located at Frankstown, Blair county, Pa.; practiced there a short time, visited Europe for his health. When he returned to the United States he settled at Mount Carmel, Illinois, and practiced medicine there until 1844, then moved to Saltsburg, Indiana county, Pa., and practiced there until his death in 1852.

Dr. *James A. Kier* was raised near West Lebanon; received a good preparatory training; studied medicine with Dr. Murray; practiced a short time in Saltsburg, then moved to Detroit, Michigan, where he resides a present.

SALTSBURG.

Dr. Robert McConnoughey, a native of Ligonier valley, was educated at the common schools and Jefferson College, Canonsburg, Pa.; studied medicine with Dr. James McConnoughey, of Mt. Pleasant; graduated at the Jefferson Medical College, Philadelphia; located in Saltsburg, Indiana county, Pa., in 1850, and practiced his profession there until his death in 1851.

Dr. Henry G. Lomison, a native of Columbia county, Pa., where he was educated at Danville Academy; clerked a short time at coal mines in Schuykill county; then went into the mercantile business in Blairsville, Pa., but soon retired from the business; studied medicine with Dr. James M. Stewart, of Indiana, Pa.; graduated at the Jefferson Medical College, Philadelphia; located in Saltsburg in 1852, and practiced there a few years, then moved to Nebraska; remained there a short time and returned to Greensburg where he resides at present.

Dr. H. S. Snowden, a native of Freeport, Armstrong county, Pa., where he was educated; studied medicine with his father, Dr. Snowden; graduated at the Philadelphia College of Medicine; located in Saltsburg in 1854 and practiced there several years, then moved to Missouri.

Dr. James Morgan, a native of Cherryhill township, Indiana county, Pa., was educated at the common schools and Blairsville Academy; studied medicine with Dr. James M. Stewart; graduated at the Jefferson Medical College; located in Maysville, Armstrong county, Pa., in 1853; practiced there two years, then moved to Saltsburg, Indiana county, and practiced there a short time, then moved to Sheffield, Bureau county, Illinois, and practiced there until his death in 1878.

Dr. Samuel T. Redick, a native of Allegheny county, received a college education; studied medicine with Dr. Daniel Boreland, of Freeport; graduated at the Jefferson Medical College, Philadelphia; located in Freeport, Armstrong county, in 1848 and practiced his profession there until 1860; then moved to Saltsburg and practiced there until 1868; then moved to Allegheny City and remained there until his death.

Dr. William McBryar, a native of Westmoreland county, Pa.; educated at the schools in the neighborhood and at Richmond Classical Institute of Jefferson county, Ohio; studied medicine with Dr. John Dickson, of Pittsburgh; graduated at the University of New York; located at New Salem, Westmoreland county, then moved to Congruity in the same county and in 1852 to Saltsburg, and in 1853 moved to Apollo where he resides at present.

Dr. William Franklin Barclay was born two miles south of Jacksonville, Indiana county; was educated at the common schools and Cherryvalley, Mechaniesburg and Jacksonville Academies and Washington and Jefferson College; taught school several terms; studied medicine with Dr. Lomison, in Greensburg, Pa. Attended a course of lectures at the Jefferson Medical College; graduated at the Long Island Hospital College, N. Y., in 1866; located in Saltsburg the same year and practiced his profession there until September, 1877, when he entered Bellevue Hospital College and Long Island College Hospital, New York. Spent a short time near Homer City, then in 1880 located in Pittsburgh, 490 Fifth avenue, now at 474 Fifth avenue, where he is engaged in active practice.

Dr. James L. Crawford was born in North Mahoning township, Indiana county, in 1842; was educated at the Covode and Glade Run Academies; studied medicine with Dr. David Alters, of Parnassus, Westmoreland county; graduated at the Jefferson Medical College, Philadelphia, in 1868 and attended a course of lectures afterwards at the Bellevue Hospital College, N. Y.; located in Saltsburg the same year and in 1874 moved to Ohio and remained there about a year, and returned to Saltsburg and practiced there until 1882. He then moved to Greensburg, and practiced there until his death, January 14, 1891. Dr. Crawford was a soldier in the late war and was a member of the Indiana County Medical Society while he was living in the county.

Dr. Thomas Carson is a native of Allegheny county, Pa.; was reared in Armstrong county, and was educated at the common schools and Eldersridge Academy; studied medicine with Dr. J. K. Parke, at Cochrans Mills, Armstrong county; graduated at the Jefferson Medical College, Philadelphia, in 1865; located in Elderton, Armstrong county, the same year and practiced his profession there until 1874, when he moved to Hulton Station, Pa., and in 1875 then moved to Saltsburg, where he resides at present.

Dr. M. R. George was born near West Lebanon, Indiana county, in 1849; he was educated at the common schools and Elderton Academy; studied medicine with Dr. Thomas Carson; graduated at the Jefferson Medical College, Philadelphia; located in Saltsburg in 1875, and practiced his profession there one year, then moved to Apollo in 1876 and practiced there until 1879; then moved to South Bend, Armstrong county, and practiced there until 1884, then moved to College Springs, Page county, Iowa, where he resides at present.

Dr. William S. Taylor, a native of Saltsburg; was educated at the public schools and Saltsburg Academy; studied medicine with Dr. J. L. Crawford; graduated at the Jefferson Medical College, Philadelphia, in 1874; located in Saltsburg and practiced his profession there until 1876; then moved to Livermore, Alameda county, California. During the year 1890 he spent in Pittsburg. He is now traveling in Europe.

Dr. Bain, a practioner from Ohio, settled in Saltsburg in 1875, remained there a short time and returned to Ohio.

Dr. Eugene H. Van Antwerp, a native of East Groveland, Livingston county, New York; was educated at the Genesee Wesleyan Seminary, at Lyma, New York; studied medicine there; graduated at the Jefferson Medical College, Philadelphia, in 1878; located in Saltsburg the same year. Returned in a short time to his native state and died a few years ago.

Dr. William B. Ansley moved from Apollo to Saltsburg in 1880, and continues to practice his profession there until the present time. (See Plumville.)

Dr. William W. Johnston, a native of Loyalhannah township, Westmoreland county; was educated at the common schools and Saltsburg Academy; studied medicine with Dr. Crawford; graduated at the Bellevue Medical College Hospital, New York, in 1881; he located in Saltsburg, the same year and practiced his profession there until 1891, then moved to Greensburg, where he resides at present.

Dr. William T. Larimer moved from West Lebanon to Saltsburg in 1883, and practiced there until 1888, then moved to Allegheny City. (See West Lebanon.)

Dr. Merchant C. Householder, a native of Washington county, was educated and studied medicine in Apollo; graduated at the Jefferson Medical College, Philadelphia, in 1888; located in Saltsburg the same year and practiced there until 1889; then moved to Washington, Pa., where he resides at present.

Dr. John Albert Barker, a native of Westmoreland county, was educated at the common schools and Saltsburg Academy; studied medicine with Dr. Ansley; graduated at the Jefferson Medical College, Philadelphia, in 1890; located in Saltsburg where he is practicing his profession.

Dr. Elias Bruce Earheart, a native of Indiana county, a graduate of Mt. Union College, taught school several terms; studied medicine with Dr. Ansley; graduated at the Cincinnati College of Medicine and Surgery of Ohio in 1890; located in Saltsburg where he is engaged in the practice of his profession.

SMICKSBURG was laid out in 1827.

Dr. Meeker settled at Glade Run, a few miles from Smicksburg at an early date. He was the physician that the early settlers of South and North Mahoning townships called upon when a physician was needed for many years. In 1829 he moved to Elderton in the same county, and a few years latter to Butler, Pa.

Dr. William N. Sims, the first physician that located in Smicksburg, was a native of Burlington, New Jersey; was educated at Uniontown, Pa.; studied medicine with Dr. Morton, of Wheeling, West Virginia; attended lectures at Richmond, Virginia; located at St.Clairsville, Ohio; practiced his profession there two years, and then moved to Pughtown, Brook county, West Virginia, remained there a short time and in 1831 moved to Glade Run, Armstrong county, Pa., and practiced his profession there until 1834, when he moved to Smicksburg, Indiana county, and remained there until his death in March 9, 1872.

Dr. James Ross, a native of Indiana borough, was educated at the Indiana Academy and Kenyon College, Ohio; studied medicine with Dr. James M. Stewart; graduated at the Jefferson Medical College, Philadelphia; located in Smicksburg in 1838 and practiced his profession there several years, then moved to Clarion, Clarion county, and practiced there until his death.

Dr. William Reed, a native of Indiana borough, was educated at the Indiana Academy; studied medicine with Dr. James M. Stewart; graduated at the Western Reserve Medical College, Cleveland, Ohio; located in Smicksburg in 1844, practiced his profession there a few years, then moved to Allegheny county; then to Beaver county and in 1856 to Indiana; went into partnership with Dr. St.Clair and remained in Indiana about three years; then moved to Ibera, Ohio. He is at Agosto, Marion county, Ohio, at present.

Dr. Barnabas Sweeny, a native of Allegheny county, Pa. After he received a good English education, he taught school for several years; then studied medicine at different times with Drs. Taylor and Stewart; practiced one year with Dr. Allison, in Elderton; then a short time with Dr. Forney, in Kittanning; located in Smicksburg, in 1857, and practiced there until 1866, when he moved to Brookville, Jefferson county, and remained there about eighteen years; then moved to DuBois, Pa., and died there in 1890.

Dr. E. D. Barrett, a native of Montgomery, Massachusetts,

was educated, studied medicine and practiced medicine several years in his native State. He then studied theology and came into the neighborhood of Smicksburg a Presbyterian minister, and labored in that capacity for a number of years, but would visit the sick in case of emergency. After spending several years in the ministry in that neighborhood, he retired from pastoral work and practiced medicine several years with success. He came to Indiana county in 1841 and moved to Springfield, Illinois, in 1859 and practiced medicine there until his death.

Dr. *Samuel D. Barrett*, a native of Massachusetts, where he received a college education, studied medicine with his father, Rev. Dr. Barrett; graduated at the Western Reserve Medical College, Cleveland, Ohio; practiced medicine several years a few miles north of Smicksburg; then moved to Shelbyville, Illinois, in 1859 and practiced there until his death.

Dr. *David R. Crawford*, a native of Eldersridge, was educated at the common schools and Eldersridge Academy; studied medicine with Dr. C. McEwen; attended lectures at Cleveland, Ohio; located at Reynoldsville, Jefferson county; practiced there a few years, then moved to Smicksburg, Indiana county, Pa., in 1865, and continues to practice in the same place.

Dr. *William E. Dodson* was born near Smicksburg, West Mahoning township, Indiana county, Pa., Sept. 8, 1854; was educated at the common schools, Dayton Academy and State Normal School, Indiana, Pa.; studied medicine with Dr. David R. Crawford; graduated at the Jefferson Medical College, Philadelphia; located in Smicksburg in the Spring of 1881, and practicing there a short time moved to Newville to assist Dr. Lowman, and in the fall of the same year located in Marion; in the fall of 1882 he moved to Richmond and secured a good practice, and remained there until the spring of 1887, then returned to Marion where he resides at present.

Dr. *James M. Patton*, a native of Kittanning, Pa., was educated at the common schools and Elderton and Glade Run

Academies; studied medicine with Dr. Deemer, of Manorville, and Dr. John M. St.Clair, of Elderton; graduated at the College of Physicians and Surgeons, of Baltimore, Maryland, in 1885; located in Smicksburg in 1885 and located at Kellys Station, Armstrong county, in 1886, and has been in regular practice in the same place up to the present time. Dr. Patton is a member of the Armstrong County Medical Society.

Dr. W. T. Crawford was raised in Smicksburg, Pa.; was educated at the Smicksburg schools and Dayton Academy; studied medicine with his father, Dr. D. R. Crawford; graduated at the Western Pennsylvania Medical College, Pittsburgh, Pa., in 1889; located in Smicksburg the same year and continues in the regular practice of his profession in that place.

Dr. Henry S. Barrett was born near Smicksburg, Indiana county, Pa., August 7, 1856; was educated at the public schools in Smicksburg, Glade Run Academy and Pennsylvania College, at Gettysburg, Pa.; taught school several terms; studied medicine with Dr. S. S. Hamilton, of Punxsutawney, Pa.; attended lectures at the Western Reserve Medical College, at Cleveland; graduated at the Toledo Medical College, Ohio; attended special courses at several hospitals in Philadelphia; passed examination by the faculty of the Medico-Chirurgical College, Philadelphia. Located at Cool Spring, Jefferson county, and practiced his profession there near six years, then moved to Smicksburg in November, 1889, and has been engaged in the practice of his profession there to the present time.

SHELOCTA was laid out in 1836.

Dr. Hugh A. Calvin, a native of Crawford county, Pa., where he was educated; studied medicine with Dr. James Dowling, of Brookville, Jefferson county, Pa.; located in Shelocta in 1841 and practiced his profession there two years; then moved to Ohio, and returned to Brookville, Pa., in 1850, and practiced there until his death a few years later. Dr. Calvin was the first settled physician in Shelocta.

Dr. Robert McChesney, a native of Mercer county, Pa.; was educated at the common schools, Jamestown Academy and Allegheny College at Meadville, Pa.; studied medicine with Dr. James Dowling, of Brookville, Pa.; graduated at the Medical College of Ohio, Cincinnati; located in Shelocta in 1843 and has continued in the regular practice of his profession in the same place to the present time.

Dr. D. Carson Rankin, a native of Beaver county, Pa.; was educated at the Beaver Academy and Westminster College; studied medicine with Dr. Robert McChesney; attended a course of lectures; located in Shelocta in 1862, and practiced there one year. In 1863 he moved to Taylorsville and practiced there a few years, then moved to Elderton, Armstrong county, Pa., where he died in 1867.

Dr. William L. Reed was born in Armstrong township, Indiana county, Pa., February 11, 1843; he was educated at the common schools, Eldersridge Academy and Westminster College; studied medicine with Dr. Robert McChesney; attended a course of lectures at the College of Physicians and Surgeons at Cincinnati, Ohio; located in Shelocta in 1869, and practiced his profession there until 1875; then moved to Jacksonville and practiced there until 1889, when he moved to Homer City, where he continues his professional work. Dr. Reed was a soldier in Co. D, 62nd Reg't. Pa. Vol., during the war, received several very severe wounds while in service. He was a member of the Legislature of Pennsylvania during the sessions of 1888 and 1889.

Dr. Thomas J. Marlin, located in Shelocta, 1870, and practiced there until 1888, and then moved to Tarkio, Missouri, where he resides at present. (See Clarksburg.)

Dr. William A. McChesney, a native of Shelocta; was educated at the borough schools; Eldersridge Academy and Westminster College; studied medicine with his father, Dr. Robert McChesney; graduated at the College of Medicine and Surgery, Cincinnati, Ohio; located in Shelocta in 1874, and has practiced his profession there to the present time.

SMITHPORT.

Dr. Benjamin C. Irwin, a native of Conemaugh township, Indiana county, Pa., was educated at Eldersridge Academy and Washington College; studied medicine with Dr. Banks; graduated at the Western Pennsylvania Medical College, Pittsburgh, Pa.; practiced a few months in Allegheny county; located in Shelocta in 1889, and remained there a few months; moved to Louisville, then to New Alexandria, Westmoreland county, Pa., where he resides at present.

Dr. Elmer E. McAdoo was born near West Lebanon, Indiana county, Pa., March 7, 1862; was educated at the common schools, Eldersridge Academy, Carrier Seminary, Clarion, Pa., Eastman College, Poughkeepsie, N. Y., and Lafayette College, Easton, Pa.; studied medicine with Dr. William Hosack and Dr. John T. Cass; graduated at the Jefferson Medical College, Philadelphia, in 1891; located in Shelocta, Indiana county, Pa., where he resides at present.

SMITHPORT was laid out in 1854.

Dr. J. Milton Shields, a native of Rayne township, Indiana county, Pa.; was educated at the common schools and Marion Institute; studied medicine with Dr. Thompson; graduated at Albany Medical College, N. Y.; located in Smithport in 1866 and practiced there one year. In 1867 he moved to Covode and practiced his profession there, with the exception of a few months in Indiana, until 1877, when he moved to New Mexico and engaged in missionary work and is still in the same kind of employment.

Dr. Henry Dickeson, a native of Armstrong county, Pa.; was educated at the Plumville schools; studied medicine with Dr. McEwen; located in Smithport in 1867 and practiced his profession there about three years, then moved to Missouri.

Dr. Joseph W. Lydick, a native of East Mahoning township, Indiana county, Pa.; was educated at the common schools and Marion Institute; studied medicine with Dr. Pitman; attended lectures at Ann Arbor, Michigan; located in Smithport in 1871, and practiced his profession there for three years, then moved to Troutville, Clearfield county, Pa., and remained there until his death.

Dr. E. Quay McHenry, a native of Washington township, Indiana county, Pa.; was educated at the common schools and Marion Institute; studied medicine with Dr. George J. McHenry; attended lectures at Ann Arbor, Michigan; located in Smithport in 1874 and practiced there about two years; then moved to DuBois, Clearfield county, Pa.; remained there a few years. He is at Rock Dale Mills, Jefferson county, Pa., at present.

Dr. George J. Reese, a native of Clarion county, Pa., where he was educated at the common schools and Reidsburg Institute, and studied medicine with Dr. Spencer; graduated at the Cincinnati College of Medicine and Surgery, Ohio; located in Smithport in 1878 and continues to practice his profession in that place.

Dr. Thomas E. Davis, a native of Cambria county, Pa., where he was educated; studied medicine with Dr. Bunn; graduated at the Jefferson Medical College, Philadelphia; located in Burnside, Clearfield county, Pa., 1867, and practiced there until 1884, when he moved to Smithport, Indiana county, Pa., where he is engaged in his profession at present.

Strongstown was laid out in 1823.

Dr. Thomas Moorhead practiced a short time in Strongstown about 1831. (See Indiana.)

Dr. Andrew A. Hamilton, a native of White township, Indiana county, Pa.; was educated at the common schools and Indiana Academy; studied medicine with Dr. Thomas St.Clair; attended a course of lectures at Western Reserve Medical College, Cleveland, Ohio; located in Strongstown in 1851 and practiced his profession there until 1855; he moved to Port Byron, Illinois, where he lived until a few years ago when he moved to Dakota.

Dr. Jasper R. Golden, a native of Indiana borough, was edacated at Freeport, Armstrong county, Pa., and studied medicine there; located in Strongstown in 1859 and practiced there about four years; then moved to Armstrong county, Pa.; a few years later he moved to Covode and died in that place.

Dr. Cicero M. Ewing, an Eclectic physician, a native of Westmoreland county, Pa., where he was educated and studied medicine; located in Strongtown in 1866 and practiced there until 1870; then moved to Greenville, and in 1873 moved to Tyrone, Blair county, Pa., where he resides at present.

Dr. Thomas J. Davison, a native of Westmoreland county, Pa., where he was educated and studied medicine; located in Strongstown in 1870 and practiced there until 1886; then moved to Ebensburg, Cambria county, Pa., where he resides at present.

Dr. J. C. Wakefield moved from Greenville to Strongstown in 1878 and practiced there about one year. (See Greenville.)

Dr. Edward H. Dickie moved from Kellysburg to Strongstown in 1887 and practiced there until July, 1891. (See Georgeville.)

Dr. Joseph Mardis, a native of Buffington township, Indiana county, Pa., was educated at the common schools; studied medicine with Dr. R. J. Tomb; graduated at the Western Pennsylvania Medical College in Pittsburgh, Pa., in 1890; located in Strongstown, where he resides at present.

TAYLORSVILLE was laid out in 1848.

Dr. James Kelly, a native of Conemaugh township, Indiana county, Pa.; was educated at the common schools and Saltsburg Academy; studied medicine with Dr. Lomison; attended a course of lectures; located in Taylorsville in 1858 and practiced there one year; then moved to Cherrytree and practiced there about three years. In 1862 he moved to Pleasant Unity, Westmoreland county, Pa., where he resides at present. Dr. Kelly was the first settled physician in Taylorsville.

Dr. Joseph F. Stewart, a native of Armstrong county, Pa.; was educated at the common schools, Jacksonville and Indiana

Academies; studied medicine with Dr. Thomas Mabon; graduated at the Jefferson Medical College, Philadelphia; located in Taylorsville in 1860; practiced there until 1862. He was appointed Hospital Stewart of 177th Regiment, Pa. Vol. In 1863 he settled in Jacksonville where he practiced his profession until his death, September 29, 1865.

Dr. George J. McHenry, a native of Washington township, Indiana county, Pa.; was educated at the common schools and Marion Institute; studied medicine with Dr. Anthony; graduated at the University of Michigan at Ann Arbor; located in Taylorsville in 1862 and practiced his profession there until 1864; then moved to Marion and practiced there until his death, July 10, 1891.

Dr. D. C. Rankin moved from Shelocta to Taylorsville in 1863 and practiced there a few years, then moved to Elderton, Armstrong county, Pa., and died in that place. (See Shelocta.)

Dr. D. Burrell, a native of Westmoreland county, Pa., where he was educated and studied medicine; attended lectures at the Cincinnati College of Medicine and Surgery, Ohio; located at New Derry in his nactive county and practiced several years. In 1866 he moved to Taylorsville and remained there two years; then moved to Homer City and practiced there three years, then returned to Westmoreland county.

Dr. John C. Morrison moved from Homer City to Taylorsville in 1867 and practiced there two years. (See Homer City.)

WHEATFIELD TOWNSHIP.

Dr. J. Gilbert Campbell practiced his profession from 1879 to 1885 in New Washington. (See Homer City).

Dr. Samuel G. Miller, a practitioner from Westmoreland county, Pa., registered in West Wheatfield township, Indiana county, Pa., in 1879.

In summoning up my sketch of the Medical Profession of Indiana County, I left out a few excrescences we always find.

The whole number of physicians that practiced in our county to this date is 270. A number of them located in different parts of the county at different periods, making the locations 346. About 102 are dead and 168 living. Some of our list can be found in different counties of our State and other States. We have 60 in regular practice at present in Indiana county. No doubt many will think strange of the omission of Medical Colleges in connection with their history. Many of the early physicians were not graduates, and a few were not even in the inside of a Medical College. When the Medical Society of the State of Pennsylvania was organized in 1848, there were only ten physicians in the county eligible to membership. When the present society was organized in 1858 there were twenty physicians in the county eligible to membership in a County Society. Many of the registered graduates were not graduates before they commenced to practice their profession. A number of them commenced to practice after attending one course of lectures and then in a few years returned to College and graduated.

In looking over the history of the medical profession of Indiana county, we have evidence of a fair proportion of high professional ability and fidelity in the discharge of their duties. Many of them were esteemed highly by the people for their professional knowledge, high moral character and devotion to duty. The profession owes the good people of Indiana county a lasting debt of gratitude for the good sound judgment they always maintained on the subject of health and life.

When they were sick they wanted a physician, not a pretender. They correctly classed new systems of medicine along with new religions. It is not long since the traveling specialist and the patent medicine vender has been able to draw the attention of the illiterate and the ignorant portion of society.

When I called the roll I had no answer from Samuel Talmage, — Reed, George Hays, John Young, Andrew Getty, George Reed, Jonathan French, — Kirkpatrick, — Simmons, — Craighead, Frank Young, — Gillespie, Samuel Duffield, — Vanhorn, P. P. Rich, Samuel F. Devlin, Benjamin F. Sterrett, Thomas Moorhead, — Gemmill, George Cleis, Samuel McKee, — Hammell, Robert K. Scott, — Campbell, Robert Ligget, David R. Allison, Samuel P. Brown, William Powell, John Hay, Hugh Adair, William G. Stewart, Hugh A. Calvin, Terrence J. Cantwell, Samuel G. Berryhill, William A. Piatt, Robert McConnoughey, Robert Mitchell, George Goodhart, Edward P. Emerson, Samuel F. Stewart, Samuel M. Ogden, John Gilpin, Robert M. S. Jackson, D. Carson Rankin, Ferdinand F. Bingell, John B. Bair, James M. Stewart, Samuel M. Elder, Henry Faulk, Augustus H. Gross, Wallace B. Stewart, Samuel W. Virtue, Joseph F. Stewart, George W. Gettys, A. H. Armstrong, James T. Adair, John Buchanan, Andrew Johnston, James Morgan, William R. Speer, Samuel T. Redick, Eugene H. Van Antwerp, Robert Barr, Herman Row, Archibald Falconer, John McFarland, R. M. Orr, D. Meeker, John McAdoo, Elisha D. Barrett, James Ross, Joseph Crooks, D. Livingston. D. Hildebrand, William McEwen, James D. Baldwin, Samuel M. Barrett, William N. Sims, John W. Crooks, Joseph W. Lydick, James D. McClure, James Shields, Joseph G. Golden, Thomas McMullen, Joseph H. Ake, J. C. Edgar, Chalmers S. McCrea, Alonza Lowman, Emanuel Brallier, David M. Marshall, Barnabas Sweeney, James G. Davis, William Altman, Joseph H. Smith, John K. Thomson, Thomas Mabon, James L. Crawford, Thomas M. Laney, Robert J. Marshall, George J. McHenry. They are not here; they have passed on; they rejoice on earth no more; they sleep well after life's fitful fever. We know that their examples are not lost on those who have taken their places in this noble county.

RESOLUTION.

Indiana, Pa., March 29, 1869.

A special meeting of the Indiana County Medical Society was convened for the purpose of taking action in regard to the death of Dr. James M. Stewart, Dr. William Anderson presiding *pro tem.*

The following preamble and resolutions were read and upon motion unanimously adopted, viz:

"Whereas, It has pleased Almighty God, the Sovereign Ruler of the Universe to call away from his sphere of honor and usefulness, our aged friend and fellow physician, James M. Stewart, M. D., therefore be it

Resolved, That while we bow in humble submission to Him who never errs, nevertheless we cannot but express our heartfelt sorrow at the decease of one who has been an honor to the profession and a benefactor to the community.

Resolved, That in the death of Dr. Stewart we have lost a Counselor in whose judgment we could all confide—the community a citizen eminently worthy of their respect and love—whose sobriety, skill, kindness and delicacy of feeling, gave evidence of those qualities of mind and heart by which all the best and most eminent of our profession have been distinguished.

Resolved, That this society in assembling to do honor to its first President, recognize in him the skillful physician, the honest, upright citizen; the kind parent and true friend; always faithful, just and kind hearted; liberal in his opinions and in his treatment of others—never actuated by narrow, jealous or unkind sentiments.

Resolved, That we tender the family and friends of the deceased our warmest sympathies for the bereavement they have suffered, but hope and trust that conscious as they must be, that he had filled up the full measure of a useful and well spent life; they have all the consolation possible in their affliction.

Resolved, That a copy of the above preamble and resolutions be presented to the family of the deceased and that the same be published in the papers of the county and entered upon the minutes of this society."

On motion society adjourned.

H. Row,   WILLIAM ANDERSON,
Secretary.   President.

Joseph F. Stewart, M. D.—1832-65. Joseph F. Stewart, M. D., died at his residence in the borough of Jacksonville, on the 29th of September, 1865, in the thirty-third year of his age. Dr. Stewart turned his early attention to the study of medicine. He was the student and finally became the successor of Thomas Mahon, M. D., an eminent physician. He finished his course of studies at the Jefferson Medical College, Philadelphia, Pa. Although his experience in the profession was but brief, he had established an extensive practice. He was respected by all who knew him for his genuine worth. He was courteous in manner, kind in disposition, religious in character, and merited the esteem of all his acquaintances. Trusting in the merits of the Saviour, he died a Christian.—*Wm. Jack.*

James T. Adair, M. D.—1836-66. James T. Adair, M. D., the subject of this brief memoir, was born in Indiana county, Pa., on the 24th of January, 1836. After receiving such an education as our common schools afforded, he pursued an academical course of study, and still later commenced the study of medicine. After eighteen months study in the office of Dr. Thomas Mahon, he attended the usual course of lectures at Jefferson Medical College, Philadelphia, Pa., graduating in the spring of 1859, and commenced the practice of his profession in Indiana. After practicing there for some time he removed to Mt. Jackson, Lawrence county, Pa., where he devoted his time assiduously to the duties of his profession until the summer of 1863, when he received the appointment of Assistant Surgeon of the 77th P. V. V. I. During the latter part of the year 1865 his regiment was stationed near San Antonia, Texas, in a malarious section of the country, where with his accumulated labors, his health gradually failed. But he preferred remaining with his regiment until they were mustered out of the service in Philadelphia on the 15th of January, 1866, when he returned to his parental home, the victim of that fell destroyer, consumption, under which he gradually sank and departed this life on the 5th day of May, 1866. Dr. Adair had a mind well stored with the medical literature of the present day, was possessed of a strong vigorous intellect and of that positive character which investigates the most obstruse and difficult subjects thoroughly. Few men had greater power of analysis and discrimination than he. A lover of truth and justice, a hater of oppression, a christian and a gentleman. Who can doubt that he is enjoying the peaceful rest which remaineth for the people of God, with the spirits of just men made perfect?—*Thomas McMullen, M. D.*

Robert Barr, M. D.—1828-82. Robert Barr, M. D., was born in Cherryhill township, Indiana county, Pa., August 3, 1828. He spent his early life on a farm and was educated at the Indiana Academy, Indiana, Pa. Studied medicine in the office of Dr. Wallace B. Stewart, in Greenville, Indiana county, and graduated at the Jefferson Medical College, Philadelphia, in 1854; located in Armagh the same year and practiced his profession in that place until 1859, when he removed to Indiana which he claimed to be his home until his death, March 2, 1882. In 1861 Dr. Barr was appointed Surgeon of the 67th Reg. Pa. Vol. and in a short time was appointed Surgeon of the Third Brigade, Third Division of Sixth Army Corps, which position he held until his term of service expired in 1864. Dr. Barr was a member of the Indiana County Medical Society, and of the Medical Society of the State of Pennsylvania. He was married in 1868 to Miss Cordelia Elder, who survives him; they had no children. His health had been declining for a number of years, but he was able to move around his home until a few weeks before his death. *W. A.*

Samuel M. Elder, M. D.—1831-68. Samuel M. Elder, M. D., was born May 17, 1831, and died June 17, 1868, being in his 38th year. He graduated at the Jefferson Medical College in

1861, and entered the army in July of the same year as a volunteer (private) in Co. H, 12th Reg., Pennsylvania Reserves. He was promoted to First Sergeant, then to Lieutenant, and then Captain. Having served three years, he returned home at the head of those of his Company who had survived the horrors of war. While attending an extra term of medical lectures he was again called and entered the army as an Assistant Surgeon. On his return at the close of the war, he located in Jacksonville, in his native county of Indiana, where he practiced his profession until failing health compelled him to relinquish it. He died at his father's house, near Armagh, of Pulmonary Consumption, induced no doubt by the exposure and fatigue incident to a life in camp and field. His life as a citizen, soldier, physician and Christian, and the respect shown him in his last illness and at his obsequies by his many friends, give ample testimony that he served his country and generation well. He died in full faith and belief of the Christian religion, expecting a glorious immortality beyond this vale. Peace to his ashes.—*Wallace B. Stewart, M. D.*

Thomas McMullen, M. D.—1826-84. The subject of this memoir descended from Scotch Highlanders. John McMullen, his grandfather, was a soldier in the Revolutionary Army; he crossed the Allegheny mountains about the year 1790 and settled a few miles southwest from the site of Indiana borough. In a short time the Indians became hostile and the few settlers were compelled to flee for safety to Franklin county, Pennsylvania. His father, Alexander McMullen, was a sergeant in Captain Gordon's company of Col. James Fenton's regiment which served in the war of 1812. He was in the battles of Chippewa, Lundy's Lane and several other engagements. He left his home in Franklin county, Pa., in 1819, and came to the farm his father had left nearly thirty years before, settled and remained there until his death in 1864.

Dr. Thomas McMullen was the third son of Alexander McMullen. His early life was spent working on the farm. After finishing the course of instruction in the common schools of the district he completed his course in the higher English and classical branches at the Blairsville Academy. He studied medicine with Dr. James McMullen, of Mechanicsburg, and graduated at Jefferson Medical College, Philadelphia. He first settled at Bells Mills, Indiana county, Pa., where he remained about eighteen months; he moved to Monmouth, Warren county, Illinois, remained there five months and returned to Pennsylvania and settled in Greenville, Indiana county, in 1857 and remained there until his death. Dr. McMullen was a successful physician and was highly respected in the community in which he lived and worked ; his practice extended over a large section of country ; his life was one of incessant toil incident to a large country practice. He was high toned and honorable with his professional brethern, conscientious and earnest with his patients, a friend of education, an exemplary citizen, a good husband, a kind father and strongly devoted to his family and friends. He was a member of the Indiana County Medical Society from its organization and a member of the Medical Society of the State of Pennsylvania since 1865. He represented Indiana county in the House of Representatives in the sessions of 1871-72. He married Rebecca J., daughter of Rev. Samuel Swan, in 1858 at that time a resident of Illinois. They had eleven children, his wife and nine children survive him. For many years he was an active and consistent member of the Presbyterian church. He suffered from irregular acton of his heart for over twenty years, and about a year before his death was threatened with paralysis, but not willing to refuse his professional services to the sick and needy, he struggled on until early in October, 1883, when his strength gave way. For some time he was hopeful that he might be able to do more good, but he gradually sank from nervous prostration until February 12, 1884, when he breathed his last aged, 58 years.— *W. A.*

George J. McHenry, M. D.—1836-91. Dr. George J. McHenry was born June 2, 1836, in Washington township, Indiana county, Pa. His early life was spent on a farm. After leaving the common schools he attended the Marion Institute, taught school, studied medicine with Dr. William Anthony in Marion, graduated at Ann Arbor Medical College, Michigan; located in Taylorsville in 1862 and practiced there about one year, then moved to Marion Center, where he practiced his profession until his death, July 10, 1891, aged 55 years. Dr. McHenry was a member of the Indiana County Medical Society for several years. He was an honest, upright and consciencious physician, true to his patients, consistent in all his professional relations. He united with the Presbyterian church when a young man and was an elder in the same body for several years. In his death the church lost a worthy member and the community a true exemplary citizen.— *W. A.*

The Medical Society of the State of Pennsylvania, was organized in Lancaster City, Pa., April 12, 1848. Dr. Samuel Humes, of Lancaster City, was elected President, and Drs. Henry S. Patterson, of Philadelphia, and George B. Kerfoot, of Lancaster, Secretaries. They adopted a Constitution and By-Laws. The second meeting of the Society was held in Reading, Pa., April 11, 1849. The Constitution and By-Laws were amended at the second meeting. The following persons were appointed a committee to address the members of the medical profession throughout the State: Drs. Edward D. Kitto, of Lycoming county, George W. Norris and Henry S. Patterson, of Philadelphia.

In the fall of 1848 there was an effort made to organize The Indiana County Medical Society. Dr. Jas. M. Stewart, of Indiana, was elected President, and Dr. Wallace B. Stewart, of Greenville, was elected Secretary. There were committees appointed to prepare a Constitution and By-Laws and Fee Bill for the Society. The committees failed to report and after two or three meetings, the organization collapsed, and for a period of ten years, there was no effort made to organize a County Medical Society. In 1858 in pursuance of notice given a number of the physicians of Indiana county, met in the borough of Indiana, on Wednesday, June 23, 1858, for the purpose of forming a County Medical Society.

Dr. Wm. Anderson called the Society to order, and moved for the purpose of temporary organization, that Dr. Jas. M. Stewart, of Indiana, be called to the chair, agreed to unanimously. Dr. Thos. St.Clair nominated Dr. Wm. Anderson, for Secretary, which was also agreed to. The physicians present gave their views on the objects and interests of a Medical organization.

On motion of Dr. Thos. St.Clair the Society was formed into The Indiana County Medical Society, passed unanimously.

The following officers were elected unanimously: President, Dr. Jas. M. Stewart, of Indiana, Vice President; Dr. Thos. McMullen, of Greenville; Secretary, Dr. William Anderson, of Indiana; Treasurer, Dr. Thos. Mabon, of Jacksonville.

The President appointed the following gentlemen a committee to prepare and report a Constitution and By-Laws at the next meeting of Society: Drs. Thos. St.Clair, Thos. Mabon and Christopher McEwen; and on fee bill, Drs. Wm. Anthony, Wm. Reed and Thos. McMullen. On motion of Dr. Mabon, Drs. James M. Stewart, Thos. St.Clair and Wm. Anderson, all of Indiana, were appointed to issue an address to the medical profession of Indiana county. The following address was issued:

At the last meeting of the Indiana County Medical Society the undersigned were appointed a committee to address the members of the profession throughout the county, calling their attention to the importance of the Society. In performing this duty, we feel that we cannot too strongly urge upon your notice a subject that appeals at once to your best interests, your professional pride, and a proper sense of what is due, both to the profession and the public. Every individual on entering the profession, as he becomes thereby entitled to its privileges and immunities, incurs an obligation to exert his best abilities to maintain its dignity and honor; to exalt its standing and extend the bounds of its usefulness. He is bound to use unwearied diligence in enriching the sciences and elevating the condition of its members.

We now put the question to every physician in the county: Have you the honor and welfare of your profession at heart? Are you willing to do your part in sustaining its honor and promoting its welfare? Shall not the profession be organized for the protection of its own interests? Shall this society, so long desired and contended for, be allowed to fail from your neglect? Shall the foundation, laid under such auspicious circumstances, crumble into ruins without an effort to raise upon it a superstructure befitting the magnitude of the cause? The importance of an organization of the medical profession is manifestly required at present. Nothing but this will preserve the character of the profession and improve its education. Nothing but this will draw the line of demarkation between the physician and the quack and save us from being confounded in the popular estimation with ignorant pretenders, whom no law prevents, from assuming the titles of the profession as a cloak for the basest charlatanism. The remedy is in ourselves. We have but to unite the profession to labor for its advancement in learning and skill, to cheer and encourage by friendly association, every honorable physician, and utterly exclude from professional intercourse all empirical and irregular practitioners. When we respect ourselves and our common art, an enlightened public will respect us for it. The members of every profession and calling, the advocates of every form of opinion, are forming associations for the advancement of their particular interests. Shall it be said that the members of our profession are too indifferent to their interests, and the cause of humanity to follow this worthy example? We know too well the liberality of our profession to doubt the result of an appeal to the better feelings of its members. It is well-known that there is not a body of men in the world, who sacrifice more on the alter of benevolence. There are none more ready to yield their immediate interests to the general good and the ultimate promotion of the cause of science and philanthrophy. All that is wanted is a determined and united effort. Let it be made and the result will be success. We would most earnestly urge every regular physician in the county to join the Medical Society without delay. You may rest assured that the beneficial consequences resulting from the society, will not be a tardy elevation of the profession. They will be felt by all of us at home and that immediately. The society will supply many of the wants of medical men by giving them opportunities of extending professional intercourse and of cultivating friendly relations. They will get to understand each other better and free them from ungenerous rivalry and jealousies, which often bring scandal on the profession. It will also afford opportunities of increasing our medical knowledge, by frequent interchange of opinion, of comparison, of observation, as well as new strength for its individual members, and which will result in public good. Why stand back longer? You are all alike responsible in sustaining and elevating our knowledge and usefulness. The next meeting of the society will be held in the borough of Indiana, on Tuesday, Sept. 28th.

There is no good reason why every regularly educated physician in the county, who is not a member should not join in with those who have thus far labored in the society. With an earnest desire to advance the most useful and profound of human pursuits."

Indiana, August 18, 1858.

July 21, 1858, society met. Committee on Constitution and By-Laws reported. Report adopted. Committee on fee bill reported. Report adopted.

Sept. 28, 1858, society met. The Secretary reported that he had complied with the requirements of the Medical Society of the State of Pennsylvania, in forwarding two copies of our Contution and By-Laws to the Censors of the district, and one copy had been returned. Approved by Daniel Leasure, George W. Allison and John Lowman, Censors.

Society then proceeded to elect two delegates to represent this society in the Medical Society of the State of Pennsylvania: Drs. Thomas Mahon and William Anderson were elected. They attended the first meeting of the State Society after their election, and were the first delegates from the Indiana County Medical Society, and the society has been annually represented since 1859.

Dr. Anderson prepared the first sanitory report for the society as follows:

Locality.—Indiana, a western county, is bounded on the north by Jefferson county, on the east by Clearfield and Cambria, on the south by Westmoreland, and on the west by Armstrong. It lies between 40° and 23' and 40° and 56' (nearly) north latitude; and 1° and 49' and 2° and 14' (nearly) west longitude from Washington City. True meridian at Indiana 1° and 26' variation west.

Hydrography.—The Conemaugh River flows along the entire south end of the county from east to west. The west branch of the Susquehanna River touches the county on the northeast. Some of the spurs of the Allegheny Mountains run into the county on the northeast. The Laurel Hill on the east, and the Chestnut Ridge entering on the south and running a northerly direction, about half the length of the county.

The dividing ridge or water-shed in the northeastern part of the county divides the waters of the Susquehanna that flow into the Chesapeake Bay, from the streams emptying into the Conemaugh and Allegheny, flowing southwestward into the Gulf of Mexico. The lowest part of this water-shed is over 1300 feet above tide. The county is well watered by numerous small streams and creeks, the largest of them, Blacklick, Yellow Creek, Two Lick, and Blacklegs, emptying into the Conemaugh; Crooked Creek, Plum Creek, Little Mahoning and Canoe, into the Allegheny; Cushion and Cush-cush into the Susquehanna.

The creeks average from 30 to 40 yards in width; those

emptying into the Conemaugh run west, those into the Allegheny northwest, and those into the Susquehanna east. The bottom lands are narrow, probably not averaging over one-fourth of a mile in width.

The streams flowing into the Conemaugh have a fall of from 20 to 30 feet to the mile, those flowing into the Allegheny from 10 to 15 feet to the mile, and those into the Susquehanna from 35 to 40 feet to the mile. Inundations are very rare. Owing to the rolling character of the surface, and the numerous small streams running nearly every point of the compass, there is very little marsh land; occasionally we see a spot of a few acres.

The western division of the Pennsylvania Canal passes through the Conemaugh Valley; the amount of lockage is about 250 feet.

Topography.—The area of the county is 775 square miles. The average altitude of the county is 1300 feet above tide. The population is about 33,000; near three-fourths of the population are the descendants of eastern Pennsylvanians, with some families from New Jersey; the balance are Scotch, Irish, German, Welsh, and their descendants. The chief avocations are agriculture, lumbering, and the manufacture of iron and salt. The principal towns are Indiana, Blairsville and Saltsburg.

Indiana, the county seat, is situated near the centre of the county, on an elevated piece of ground, about 1320 feet above tide, with 1500 inhabitants. Blairsville, 16 miles south of Indiana, on the border of the county, with 1000 inhabitants. Saltsburg, 20 miles southwest of Indiana, with 600 inhabitants.

The surface is rolling, cut into small valleys and hills by the numerous small streams; along the larger streams the valleys are also very narrow. The principal eminences are elevated hills called "round tops" throughout the county; the ascent of these elevations is from 15° to 25°, rising from 300 to 500 feet above the general surface of the county; the summits of these are from 100 square feet to one or two acres. On the top the surface is composed of sand and pebbles, with occasional sandstone rocks. None of the surface is destitute of vegetation; about one-half of the surface is cleared; the other half covered with forest. About one-third of the improved land is in grass; the balance produces wheat, rye, corn, buckwheat, oats, barley, beans, peas, potatoes, turnips, pumpkins, &c., &c.

In about one-fourth of the county—the eastern part—the timber is principally white pine and spruce; the balance of the county is covered with white oak, black oak, chestnut oak, red oak, poplar, chestnut, hickory, sugar maple, walnut, cherry, locust, cucumber, &c., &c. Clearing off the forest has made our summers more dry, and our winters more changeable.

GEOLOGY.—But little attention has been paid to the geology of Indiana county. The present report will necessarily be meagre, and perhaps in some particulars imperfect; but we give it as far as we have data.

Indiana county belongs to the ninth district of the general palæozoic region of the State. It comprizes only the vespertine, umbral, and seral series. The former in very narrow lines of outcrop; bordering and dividing some of the coal basins. The coal basins are bordered generally by the seral conglomerate.

The different formations dip southwest.

Vespertine.—This formation, as seen in the county, is a coarse gray sandstone, engirding each basin by a continuous belt of rocks. At the gap of the Laurel Hill, on the Conemaugh, it is visible on the north side of the river for several hundred feet; thickness supposed to be about 400 feet.

On the Conemaugh, at the western slope of the Chestnut Ridge, this formation is a gray argillaceous and micaceous sandstone, with a few beds of dark shale; thickness about 350 feet.

In anticlinal belts of the Chestnut Ridge this formation occupies the higher flanks, and even the summits of the mountains which sustain the seral conglomerate, and the coal measures at a subordinate elevation on their slopes.

The rate of diminution of this deposit is nearly due west.

Umbral Red Shales.—This formation, at the Conemaugh gap, contains seral, loose, coarse, and fine pebbly sandstone. Red and green marl alternating, red predominant, including a few sandy layers, 35 feet; gray fine-grained sandstone, 5 or 6 feet; impure white ore from 1 to 3 inches; alternating green and red shale, bands of sandstone including 6 inches coarse ore, 17 feet; argillaceous sandstone, 3 feet; red shale and green argillaceous sandstone, 3 feet; red shale cutting out coarse gray sandstone, 10 feet; red and green shales and argillaceous sandy beds, 8 feet; calcareous sandstone, 10 to 12 feet; red sandy limestone, 3 feet; light bluish-gray sandy limestone, thick bedded and very oblique, 40 feet.

At the western slope of the Chestnut Ridge it consists of red marly shales, containing little gray sandstones in the upper half; centrally a thick bed of sandy limestone; and composed in its lower part of olive shales, thickness 195 feet. This formation occupies a sort of elevated terrace on the mountains a little below their actual tops, with a gentle depression, so that the vespertine conglomerate is brought nearer the true coal rocks, and forms with the seral conglomerate, but one general rim or border to the several basins. In some parts it would seem not to be overlaid by any conglomerate, but is succeeded by coal measures.

Seral.—This formation generally caps the highest summits or crests of the table lands, and has the same peculiarity as in coal measures elsewhere in the State.

Two and a half miles from Campbell's Mill, on Blacklick Creek, the following section was had: Unknown to the top of the hill, 40 feet; sandstone, 40 feet; unknown, 20 feet; sandstone, 17 feet; red argillaceous strata; sandstone, 4 feet; slate and shale, 10 to 15 feet; unknown, 20 to 30 feet; red argillaceous shale, containing small bivalves; red argillaceous stratum, bluish in spots, 8 feet; light green fossiliferous limestone, 10 inches; 20 feet to the creek not exposed. Nearly opposite this section nodular hematic ore in very red shale may be observed.

Near the mouth of Blacklick Creek the following section was obtained: Olive slate, 20 feet; blue slate; unknown, 15 feet; calcerous clay, 2½ feet; red and green shales, 6 feet; green shale, 10 feet; unknown, 25 feet; green fossiliferous sandstone, 10 inches; unknown, 10 feet; red shale, 3 feet; to the level of the creek, 54 feet.

Above the forks of Twolick, 35 or 40 feet above the level of the stream, the following section was obtained: Argillaceous limestone, studded with bivalves imperfectly preserved, 6 inches; compact limestone, with fewer fossils, 4 inches; green and red shales, in colored bands, 10 to 12 inches; green fossiliferous limestone, 10 inches; greenish sandstone, 5 inches; red shale, 2 feet; dark blue slate.

In boring a well in Indiana, 1325 feet above tide, 340 feet above Blairsville, 50 feet above the beds of the rivulets on each side; one south about 100 perches, the other west 80 perches; about 50 feet below the red shale in the immediate neighborhood: Well 162 feet deep—bore 2½ inches—digging in gravel and hard slate rock, 17½ feet; hard slate rock, of a dark blue color, 8 feet; soft slate rock, of a dark blue color, 40½ feet; soft slate rock, in which was a vein of water, 19 feet; at 75 feet, the water sunk to 33 feet from the top of the well; red shale mixed with a yellowish-green sandstone and slate, very soft, with a vein of water, 7 feet; in this shale the water sank to 43½ feet from the surface; black slate, pretty hard, 4 feet; white flint, very hard, 4 inches; at this stage of boring the water sank to 53 feet 10 inches from top of the well; dark colored hard slate, with a mixture of white, 2 feet; blue clay, with a little sand, 4 feet 6 inches; water, 54 feet from top of the well; hard gray sandstone rock, 2 feet 6 inches; light blue slate and white clay, very soft, 4 feet; dark gray fine-grained slate, with very little sand, 5 feet; dark blue slate, with a few thin shales of whitish colored slate, 18 feet; black slate, not very hard, 16 feet; soft black slate, 1 foot 3 inches; hard slate, 2 feet; gray sandstone, 5 feet 6 inches; black slate, very hard, 3 feet 3 inches.

Coal.—The 2nd and 3d, and a small portion of the 4th basins of the bituminous coal region underlie Indiana county. The coal formation dips southwest with symmetrical flexures.

At Centreville, near the middle of the 2nd basin, only the upper coal and limestone are out of the water. Coal 6 feet thick emerges half a mile above the village; the same vein is seen one and a half miles below the village.

Two other coal seams, supposed to be of the barren series, appear north of Bolivar, in the hills—the third measure is 4 feet thick. Following the basin to the northeast, the same measures have been worked at various points. In the neighborhood of Strongstown, the first coal vein measures 4 feet; then strata 100 feet. Second vein, 3 feet thick, 50 feet higher. Third vein 18 inches thick, then 30 feet strata. Fourth vein 18 inches thick. There are only two coal seams exposed on the Conemaugh in the third basin, each underlaid by a bed of limestone; they crop out at the axes of the Chestnut Ridge.

The upper Freeport coal has been worked in the northern and northeastern half of the county, several beds on Twolick Creek and Yellow Creek: On Dixon's Run, Buck Run, Rayne's Run, Pine Run, near the village of Marion Center; on Crooked Creek, near Chambersville; on McKee's Run, 4½ miles north of Indiana, this bed is coal 22 inches; grayish-black crumbly shale, from 8 to 10 inches; coal, 4 feet 6 inches—the roof a gray micaceous sandstone; dip north 30 degrees W.; it contains sulphate of iron—the same is seen in many other places to the northeast. The other veins average from 3½ feet to 5 feet, all underlaid with limestone, and some of them roofed with slate and iron ore.

On Little Mahoning Creek, at Robertsville, the upper Freeport coal is seen—the same is seen four miles west. At Diltz's Mill there is a thin vein of coal, supposed to be the same. At Ewing's Mill, shale and thin coal seams are opened.

At Kinter's Mill, on Little Mahoning, where the 3d axis crosses the Mahoning Valley, the upper Freeport coal is opened above the level of the stream, and a 6 inch vein of the barren measure is seen above, with calcareous shales.

From Mahoning south to the Conemaugh, the beds are the common ones of the basin, occurring at the level of most of the small streams, while the hills are composed of the unproductive high measures.

We also find coal measures, superficial and thin, until they cease to be continuous, prolonged by a few scattered patches, leaping from summit to summit of the narrow synclinal table-lands.

At Smicksburg, in the 4th basin, the upper and lower Freeport coal seams are opened. The upper vein is 4½ feet thick; the strata between the upper and lower average about 50 feet. The lower bed has been opened at various points, measuring 2½ feet.

Between the terminus of the Chestnut Ridge and the water-shed between the eastern and western waters, the coal seams are split and very irregular in many places. The same is observed in spots on the borders of the 3d and 4th basins.

In 100 parts of Blairsville coal, there is as follows: Volatile matter, 31; carbon, 69; earthy matter, 4. Laminated columnar, hard, compact, shining jet black.

Ten miles southwest, and about the same distance west from Indiana, the great Pittsburgh coal seam caps the highest knolls between the streams; sinking deeper and deeper under overlying rocks, until, 3½ miles west of Saltsburg, 175 feet of upper barren measures overlie it, containing two unimportant coal seams.

The Pittsburgh coal vein is seen on the north side of Twolick; half a mile north of Blacklick it is 7 feet thick.

Southeast of Twolick and one and a half miles north of Blacklick, a 7 foot coal bed, parted by bands of slate, has been opened.

In the neighborhood of West Lebanon, the same vein is opened in the higher hills. Near M'Means, on Blacklegs Creek, the vein is 11 feet thick.

West of Indiana there is a third axis, brought up in all the creeks, which affords an abundance of both fuel and lime. This coal has been opened at Jacksonville, and various other points in that neighborhood; the vein averages about 3½ feet.

There is a barren measure overlying the Pittsburgh coal seam of 500 feet.

The barren measure between the upper Freeport coal and Pittsburgh coal is from 450 feet to 500 feet.

Limestone accompanies all the coal measures in the county; in some places the limestone is but a few feet under the coal; in other places from 20 to 30 feet.

In the barren measure between the upper Freeport and Pittsburgh coals there is fossiliferous limestone; in some parts of the county it has been used for various purposes; the veins average from 2 to 5 feet thick.

Iron Ore.—Bands of iron ore are found in various parts of the county. Several furnaces have been in operation on Blacklick Creek, Laurel Run, and Mahoning Creek, near Smicksburg, for several years.

At Blairsville, the ore in 100 parts contains carbonate of iron 67.20; peroxide of iron, 7.48; carbonate of lime, 3.24; carbonate of magnesia, 1.50; silica, 12.34; water, 8.0. Metallic iron in 100 parts, 37.24; dove color, smooth, nodular.

At a bank southeast of Blairsville, the following was obtained in 100 parts: Carbonate of iron, 37.80; carbonate of zinc, 5.50; carbonate of magnesia, 7.50; silica and insoluble matter, 37.80; alumina, 7.60; water, 3.50. Metallic iron in 100 parts, 18.27. The ore is mottled red and green nodular, somewhat spathose.

On the west side of the Chestnut Ridge, the following was found: Peroxide of iron, 51.25; oxide manganese, a trace; carbonate of lime, 2.00; silica and insoluble matter, 36.50; alumina, 5.96; water, 4. Metallic iron in 100 parts, 35.87. Cinnamon brown, nodular.

At Ewing's Mill, on Little Mahoning Creek, there is a vein of very pure carbonate of iron, 18 inches thick, in layers of 4 or

5 inches thick, with concretions of silica; while masses and veins of apparently pure carbonate of lime subdivide the ore.

At Robertsville there is bog ore. The above are the only beds analyzed, but in the surface of the county ore is abundant.

It is believed that the ore generally in the county would average about 30 per cent. metallic iron.

Organic Remains.—Many have been found in the county; but few persons have paid any attention to either name or classification.

The Fern has been found in abundance. In the northern part of the county the Neuropterus minor, and the Allethopterus pennsylvaniaca 1st and 2nd have been found. One place in a coal seam the Modiola. In many quarries there have been reptilian footprints discovered.

The soil in the eastern part of the county is loam and sand, as far as the pine timber extends; in the balance of the county the soil is loam and slate, with a clayey admixture in spots. The subsoil is clay and slate. The subjacent rock is a peculiar hard blue micaceous sandstone in the low land. In the higher table-lands it is variegated blue and red.

The water used for domestic purposes throughout the county is generally obtained from springs, which are very numerous; and from most of them a strong current of pure water flows throughout the year, very seldom affected by the dryest season

In the towns and villages the water is generally obtained by digging or boring wells to the depth of from 15 to 30 feet—some of them are effected in dry seasons. There are a few wells in Indiana bored to the depth of 200 feet. But very few pipes of any kind are used as conduits.

In the Conemaugh Valley there are numerous salt wells, from which are annually manufactured large quantities of salt of a very superior quality; the wells are bored to the depth of from 700 to 1000 feet; the water is pumped up with steam engines, and boiled in large kettles or pans. The yield is variable. At first it yields in 50 or 60 gallons of water a bushel of salt.

After pumping for a length of time the yield is less, requiring one hundred gallons or upwards to produce a bushel of salt.

Several springs in the county are thought to possess medicinal properties, but from the limited knowledge of their ingredients we will pass them for the present.

METEOROLOGY.—Very little attention has been paid to this subject within the last few years. With some difficulty I have obtained a thermometrical table, kept 1300 feet above tide; and a barometric table, for a few months, kept 980 feet above tide.

Thermometrical Observations.

FEBRUARY, 1859.

D.o'M	5 A.M.	12 M	6 P.M.	9 P.M.	Winds	Remarks
1	22°	50°	35°	33°	W	Clear
2	34	38	34	31	E	Cloudy
3	34	36	26	25	W	Snow five inches
4	18	26	30	18	W	Showers of snow
5	10	31	28	26	S	Clear
6	27	29	25	19	N	Light snow showers
7	11	32	25	23	E	Clear
8	24	40	32	33	E	Clear; even'g th'r'tn'g
9	31	40	33	29	E	Snow and rain
10	15	22	16	15	N	Snow showers
11	14	26	19	21	E	Snow
12	26	31	25	21	N W	Snow
13	17	...	21	20	W	Cloudy
14	14	35	31	38	E	Clear
15	40	42	41	43	E	Rain all day
16	39	52	40	34	W	Clear, pleasant
17	35	36	42	36	E	Light rain and snow
18	38	36	38	38	S W	Light rain and snow
19	35	48	48	50	E	Heavy rain at night
20	60	56	32	30	S to N W	Cloudy, windy
21	25	27	29	25	N W	Stormy, clear
22	26	51	41	37	E	Clear
23	37	60	53	50	S E	Clear, pleasant
24	38	44	33	30	N W	Clouds and sunshine
25	33	27	33	25	N E	Heavy snow all day
26	33	42	36	34	S to W	Clear p. m.
27	31	55	51	48	E	Rain at night
28	33	38	31	29	N W	Cloudy; cool

MARCH, 1859.

D.o'M	5 A.M.	12 M	6 P.M.	9 P.M.	Winds	Remarks
1	21°	41°	30°	23°	N W	Clear, cool
2	13	37	32	28	N E	Clear, cool
3	30	34	33	34	E	Rain and sleet
4	35	38	36	33	W	Snow and rain
5	30	36	36	33	W	Snow
6	27	50	47	40	E	Clear, pleasant
7	40	49	40	41	E	Cloudy
8	43	44	36	36	W	Rain all day
9	33	49	41	37	W	Clouds. Clear
10	32	56	50	48	E	Clear
11	42	63	57	57	E	Rain at night
12	49	59	52	47	S to W	Drying winds
13	35	67	54	53	W to E	Pleasant
14	51	50	52	57	E	Pleasant
15	43	43	37	36	W	Spits of snow
16	30	51	47	39	E	Clear
17	42	63	60	54	E	Cloudy
18	54	59	48	44	W	Rain all day
19	30	32	30	28	W	Snow, stormy
20	27	43	38	31	W	Clouds
21	28	61	57	53	E	Clouds
22	51	51	51	43	E	Rain part of day
23	30	64	55	52	W	Stormy
24	55	57	62	56	E	Light snow
25	38	43	38	36	W	Rain all night
26	27	36	34	31	N W	Clear, warm
27	38	62	49	46	S to W	Wet, cold
28	47	79	64	58	S E	Pleasant
29	57	56	44	40	N W	Pleasant
30	30	52	45	39	N W	Snow showers
31	29	45	40	35	N to E	Snow showers

SANITARY REPORT.

*Vegetation one month in advance of May, 1858. Less rain and more heat the present month than in May, 1858.

Thermometrical Observations—Continued.

APRIL, 1859.

D.ofM.	5 A.M.	12 M	6 P.M	9 P.M	Winds	Remarks
1	31°	65°	55°	52°	S	Clear, pleasant
2	45	61	55	52	E	Cloudy, warm
3	52	63	51	45	W	High wind
4	31	42	34	32	N W	Cloudy, cool
5	28	34	39	37	N W	Cloudy, snow
6	25	45	31	36	N W	Clear, cold
7	32	54	46	37	S	Cloudy, snow
8	35	38	33	26	N W	Heavy snow
9	19	53	45	45	E	Clear, pleasant
10	37	48	41	40	E	Rain all day
11	47	71	75	49	E	Rain storm
12	49	71	63	59	S W	Clear
13	56	69	67	63	S	Cloudy
14	65	73	54	47	S W	Flying clouds
15	37	63	61	46	E	Partly clear
16	32	37	28	36	S W	Snow
17	30	42	37	33	W	Cloudy, cool
18	34	43	43	38	W	Cloudy, cool
19	32	52	49	43	W to E	Cloudy, snow
20	38	48	46	43	S W	Cloudy, cool
21	35	63	54	46	W	Clear
22	39	52	49	49	N W	Rain all day
23	34	34	33	33	W	Four inches snow
24	29	49	48	45	S W	Clear
25	44	64	55	55		Clear
26	52	60	59	45	E	Heavy rain
27	47	50	44	53	E	Heavy rain
28	35	62	60	55	E	Clear, warm
29	34	70	68	54	S E	Clear, warm
30	48	79	74	68	S W	Clear, warm

MAY, *1859.

D.ofM.	5 A.M.	12 M	6 P.M	9 P.M	Winds	Remarks
1	50°	76°	73°	64°	E	Clear
2	59	84	75	66	S	Clear
3	60	84	97	63	S W	Clear part of day
4	49	83	65	65	E	Clear
5	59	86	77	67	E	Clear
6	56	90	83	71	E	Clear
7	61	92	77	73	E & W	Clear
8	63	91	80	73	S E	Thunderstorm
9	71	91	67	64	W	Rain all day
10	63	59	54	50	S E	Cloudy
11	50	58	57	40	E	Changeable
12	50	69	72	65	S W	Clear all day
13	63	88	75	67	E	Clear all day
14	58	80	66	55	S	Clear all day
15	50	78	66	53	N	Changeable
16	54	73	63	56		Rain and thunder
17	54	66	64	63	E	Variable
18	59	78	68	65	E	Heavy rain
19	59	65	57	65	E	Changeable
20	60	89	79	73	S E	Thunderstorms
21	63	84	71	60	E	Flying clouds
22	57	69	67	55	W	Clear
23	49	75	64	48	E	Clear
24	49	88	78	90	S E	Clear
25	50	88	70	70	E	Clear
26	58	89	78	78	E	Heavy storm
27	69	86	70	58	E	Rain and sunshine
28	49	67	67	57	E	Rain at night
29	57	77	68	63	S W	Cloudy
30	59	88	70	60	W	Clear, warm
31	60	70	62	61	E	

Thermometrical Observations—Continued.

JUNE,* 1859.

D.of M.	5 A.M	12 M.	6 P.M.	9 P.M.	Winds.	Remarks.
1	61°	78°	68°	65°	E	Cloudy. Clear
2	63	86	67	65	E	Thunderstorm
3	68	81	62	34	S to E	Clouds and sunshine
4	43	48	40	31	N E	Clouds and sunshine
5	27	61	52	52	N W	Frost and ice
6	45	73	70	57	S E	Warm
7	49	81	79	70	E	Warm
8	64	80	75	56	S E	Thunderstorm
9	44	69	69	63	S W	Cool day
10	44	56	68	44	S W	Cloud and sunshine
11	30	65	50	49	E	Cool, frosty m'rn'ng
12	50	76	72	65	W	Mild, cool air
13	52	78	75	71	E	Rain all day
14	69	82	80	70	S W	Rain part of day
15	68	85	71	69	E	Thunderstorm
16	65	73	68	56	V'r'le	Flying clouds
17	69	75	65	60	E	Rain part of day
18	50	72	64	53	S W	Clear
19	48	68	64	61	W	Heavy rain
20	63	79	74	65	E	Shower at night
21	64	80	72	61	V'r'le	Flying clouds
22	65	79	68	60	E	Flying clouds
23	61	84	61	61	S W	Heavy rain P. M.
24	57	76	67	65	W	Thundershower
25	56	76	71	62	S E	Dense fog
26	58	80	77	68	S E	Cloudy
27	68	89	74	77	S E	Clear
28	76	98	82	79	S E	Thunderstorm A.M
29	76	92	71	69	S E	Thunderstorm P.M.
30	59	95	69	62	N W	Cloudy

*June 5, frost, with ice on low lands from one-half to three-quarters of an inch in thickness, killing a great deal of grain, vegetables, and timber; making the woods look as though they had been scorched by intense heat.

JULY, 1859.

D.of M.	5 A.M.	12 M.	6 P.M.	9 P.M.	Winds.	Remarks.
1	52°	84°	80°	75°	E	Clear and Cloudy
2	74	91	72	58	Var'le	Thunderstorm
3	50	92	52	60	Var'le	Rain A. M.
4	41	76	68	62	E	Clear, cool
5	43	79	72	62	E	Clear, cool
6	52	66	60	59	S W	Rain all day
7	52	77	74	65	E	Cloudy day
8	60	82	79	70	S W	Foggy and cloudy
9	62	87	82	78	E	Clear
10	63	89	79	66	E	Clear
11	66	96	85	75	W	Clear
12	68	100	88	81	S W	Clear and warm
13	70	98	87	80	W	Clear and warm
14	72	78	74	62	W	Heavy rain
15	71	88	80	73	N W	Clear
16	70	95	88	79	E	Clear and sultry
17	68	98	88	78	S	Clear and sultry
18	62	88	75	68	S E	Clear and rainy
19	66	88	72	59	W	Rain, sunshine
20	60	78	76	68	W	Rainy evening
21	58	75	68	54	W	Clear, cool
22	60	79	67	58	E	Rain P. M.
23	58	75	68	54	W	Clear, cool
24	52	80	73	67	Var'le	Clear, cool
25	54	88	76	68	E	Clear, cool
26	50	79	72	60	E	Flying clouds
27	50	73	65	59	E	Quite cool
28	49	69	70	60	N W	Cloudy, cool
29	49	74	75	60	N W	Cloudy, cool
30	59	85	80	72	W	Clouds, sunny
31	69	82	68	—	E	Shower P. M.

SANITARY REPORT.

Thermometrical Observations.—Continued.

AUGUST, 1859.

D of M	5 A.M.	12 M	6 P.M	9 P.M	Winds	Remarks
1	67°	68°	72°	68°	E	Thunder shower
2	65	85	78	69	S E	Thunder shower
3	67	90	81	72	S E	Thunder shower
4	77	82	75	64	S E	Heavy rain
5	67	80	76	68	S W	Heavy rain
6	53	81	75	66	W	Clear, pleasant
7	60	86	75	68	S E	Clear, pleasant
8	54	88	78	75	S E	Clear, pleasant
9	62	90	84	78	E	Very warm
10	78	93	86	79	E	Very warm
11	69	95	79	73	E	Cloudy
12	65	80	75	70	E	Heavy rain
13	66	80	79	69	E	Cloudy and cool
14	62	87	81	78	E	Clear and warm
15	63	93	79	69	V'r'ble	Rain P. M.
16	63	83	72	68	E	Distant thunder
17	61	77	69	62	E	Clear
18	52	85	75	62	E	Clear
19	61	81	69	53	W	Rain and sunshine
20	52	76	66	60	W	Clear, cool
21	49	80	69	60	E	Clear, cool
22	59	80	75	70	E	Clear, cool
23	62	80	74	70	E	Clear part of day
24	68	83	76	67	E	Rain
25	66	79	70	67	S E	Flying clouds
26	62	68	67	63	E	Heavy rain
27	62	78	69	63	W	Cloudy
28	55	71	60	53	N W	Clear, cool
29	39	69	61	55	N W	Frost. Clear, cool
30	43	73	69	60	E	Clear, pleasant
31	55	77	67	60	E	Cl'r A.M., cl'dy P.M.

NOVEMBER, 1859.

D of M	5 A.M.	12 M	6 P.M	9 P.M	Winds	Remarks
1	25°	40°	39°	32°	W	Cloudy
2	28	40	49	35	E	Clear, pleasant
3	27	63	49	52	E	Clear, pleasant
4	53	71	65	61	S	Clear, pleasant
5	57	72	66	57	X	Clear, pleasant
6	39	60	58	42	W	Clear, pleasant
7	34	59	59	45	E	Claer, pleasant
8	41	60	59	53	E	Clear, pleasant
9	43	70	59	52	E	Clear, pleasant
10	59	70	60	53	S E	Part of the day clear
11	35	55	46	39	S	Flying clouds
12	35	46	49	32	N W	Heavy rain
13	36	55	25	31	E	Snow storm
14	18	29	27	21	N W	Clear, cold
15	26	45	35	33	N	Clear, cold
16	39	58	45	44	E	Clear, pleasant
17	39	72	49	50	S E	Clear, pleasant
18	40	70	40	49	S E	Clear, pleasant
19	44	48	41	39	E	Heavy rain
20	34	34	34	29	E	Clear afternoon
21	30	40	53	42	N E	Heavy rain
22	45	56	78	48	E	Clear, cool
23	37	48	36	29	E	Clear, cool
24	36	48	35	27	E	Clear, cool
25	36	35	35	41	E	Rain
26	45	54	43	41	E	Clear, pleasant
27	30	45	35	35	E	Clear A. M.
28	27	50	33	27	E	Pleasant
29	20	45	57	40	N W	Clear
30	37	65	73	55	S	Clear A. M.

Thermometrical Observations—Continued.

DECEMBER, * 1859.
*Mean temperature 25°.

D.ofM.	5 A.M.	12 M.	6 P.M.	9 P.M.	Winds.	Remarks.
1	60°	69	62	50°	S	Heavy rain
2	51	49	35	22	S	Heavy rain
3	18	21	19	17	N W	Snow and sleet
4	35	40	37	34	N E	Wet and cool
5	34	49	35	36	S E	Warm
6	41	45	51	50	S E	Rain
7	26	21	23	11	E	Snow and cold
8	9	16	8	4	E	Snow and cold
9	7	23	35	23	E	Snow and cold
10	22	23	19	14	E	Snow and cold
11	22	34	33	22	W	Snow and cold
12	27	33	14	9	N W	Cloudy
13	20	24	20	22	W	Cloudy
14	26	34	26	21	S W	Heavy snow storm
15	17	22	17	11	W	Clear, cool
16	17	43	30	25	N	Clear, cool
17	28	35	34	37	E	Heavy sleet storm
18	32	36	32	32	W	Snow
19	30	36	31	31	N	Snow
20	36	37	28	24	S E	Snow
21	20	21	15	14	E	Cold
22	10	19	14	14	S E	Snow, cold
23	12	14	9	11	W	Cold
24	9	11	9	8	N W	Stinging cold
25	7	33	30	40	S	Clear, pleasant
26	40	42	37	30	S	Clear, pleasant
27	25	33	27	21	N E	Cloudy
28	17	21	11	10	E	Cloudy
29	13	30	12	28	E	Snow and sleet
30	25	30	23	20	S W	Flying clouds
31	1	8	3	4	W	Clear

JANUARY, 1860.

D.ofM.	5 A.M.	12 M.	6 P.M.	9 P.M.	Av'ge.	Winds.	Remarks.
1	10°	14°	3°	–5	8°	W	Clear
2	–3	11	3	0	4	W	Clear in part
3	2	21	21	22	16	S E	Snowing
4	21	28	15	9	18	S E	Heavy storm
5	5	28	30	28	15	S E	Clear, cool
6	12	23	30	40	23	S	Snow. East rain
7	35	43	42	38	40	E	East rain
8	28	42	38	42	36	S E	Cloudy
9	35	42	42	51	42	S E	Clear, warm
10	50	48	48	29	48	S	Cloudy, warm
11	51	42	31	21	36	N E	Heavy rain
12	20	34	20	28	23	E	Cloudy
13	19	32	29	34	27	E	Clear
14	31	34	35	34	33	E	Cold, rain
15	30	33	34	35	32	E	Snow
16	36	36	37	26	36	S	Soft, cloudy
17	32	32	28	27	30	S	Soft, cloudy
18	36	36	28	25	30	S	Rain and snow
19	21	28	27	46	25	E	Part of day cloudy
20	30	47	45	41	42	E	Clear, pleasant
21	40	59	45	31	48	E	Clear, pleasant
22	32	43	34	33	35	E	Clear, pleasant
23	25	40	33	35	32	W	Clear, pleasant
24	38	60	56	26	52	S E	Cloudy
25	27	40	36	32	38	W	Clear
26	24	27	36	32	23	E	Heavy snow
27	27	28	22	22	24	E	Snow
28	20	28	20	21	24	W	Snow
29	10	41	25	24	39	W	Clear
30	43	40	37	41	39	N W	Clear
31	37	30	14	10	22	W	Snow storm

Thermometrical Observations.—Continued.

FEBRUARY, 1860.

D.OfM.	5 A.M.	12 M.	6 P.M.	9 P.M.	Av'ge.	Winds.	Remarks.
1	0°	9°	3°	-3°	4°	N W	Clear
2	3	19	3	19	11	E to W	Snow
3	2	19	16	15	13	E	Clear
4	19	41	20	21	25	E	Clear
5	20	25	25	27	24	E	Sleet and snow
6	42	45	41	24	40	S E	Rain
7	30	35	27	22	28	S	Snow
8	22	60	32	32	36	S	Clear
9	30	48	45	28	37	S W	Pretty clear
10	9	26	15	10	15	W	Clear
11	13	26	25	17	20	W	Clear
12	14	28	20	24	21	W	Rain P M.
13	32	58	44	40	43	W	R in P M.
14	40	39	36	32	36	W	Cloudy
15	25	26	29	32	28	N E	Snow
16	20	20	19	9	17	N W	Cloudy
17	3	22	15	15	13	E	Clear
18	20	26	28	19	23	S to S W	Snow
19	10	14	11	8	10	E	Cloudy
20	15	48	34	37	33	E	Clear
21	35	59	47	46	47	E	Clear
22	39	62	64	61	31	E	Rain
23	45	55	43	39	45	E	Cloudy
24	27	30	26	25	27	N W	Snow
25	19	26	24	24	23	E	Clear
26	15	47	35	34	32	E	Clear
27	40	62	55	51	52	S	Clear
28	40	63	55	54	53	S E	Clear
29	50	66	55	58	57	S E	Clear

MARCH, 1860.

D.OfM.	5 A.M.	12 M.	6 P.M.	9 P.M.	Av'ge.	Winds.	Remarks.
1	53°	50°	49°	43°	48°	S E	Rain
2	37	53	51	46	46	S W	Clear
3	51	53	51	53	52	S E	Rain
4	32	48	37	32	37	S W	Clear
5	31	65	55	51	50	S E	Clear
6	49	67	56	25	56	S	Clear
7	58	72	60	56	61	S W	Showery
8	51	55	48	43	48	N	Cloudy
9	30	40	28	23	30	W	Snow
10	18	24	23	22	21	W	Snow
11	25	48	37	38	36	N W	Smoky
12	34	33	24	22	28	N W	Clear
13	12	32	25	22	23	W	Clear
14	14	45	30	24	28	S E	Clear
15	25	55	51	42	43	S E	Clear
16	36	62	53	43	48	S E	Clear
17	37	71	58	50	54	S E	Cloudy
18	45	58	58	51	50	S E	Rain
19	45	52	48	48	48	W	Snow
20	38	40	31	32	35	N W	Clear
21	31	36	29	28	31	N W	Clear
22	20	32	37	32	32	N W	Cloudy
23	35	47	40	37	39	N W	Snow
24	32	35	30	28	31	W	Showery
25	20	35	24	22	25	W	Showery
26	21	36	31	29	29	W	Clear
27	15	43	35	33	31	W	Cloudy
28	30	52	32	36	37	W	Clear
29	32	57	48	45	45	W	Clear
30	41	68	59	55	56	W	Clear
31	52	78	65	60	63	W	Clear

Thermometrical Observations.—Continued.

APRIL, 1860.

D of M	5 A.M.	12 M	3 P.M.	9 P.M.	Av'ge.	Winds	Remarks
1	56	45	34	31	41	N W	Rain and snow
2	22	38	32	27	29	N	Clear
3	31	58	50	48	46	S E	Snow three in.
4	40	60	58	55	53	S E	Rain & thunder
5	40	56	43	35	43	W	Light snow
6	32	49	36	34	37	W	Clear
7	30	63	55	53	50	E	Pretty clear
8	40	80	70	68	64	E	Thunder storm
9	57	72	55	57	60	W	Thunder & rain
10	48	60	52	48	54	E	Cloudy
11	45	55	40	35	44	N E	Rain
12	30	55	50	46	45	S W	Thunder & rain
13	38	49	49	47	47	N W	Clear
14	45	37	33	25	35	N W	Snow
15	18	52	50	43	41	W	Freezing
16	40	48	54	53	48	E	Cloudy
17	61	73	56	44	59	E	Clear
18	29	36	52	48	46	W	Clear
19	38	65	52	50	51	E	Threatening
20	53	66	68	65	63	E	Rain
21	63	66	69	60	63	W	Rain
22	50	64	57	52	55	S	Rain
23	42	48	43	41	42	S E	Clear
24	29	44	34	33	35	E	Snow
25	32	38	33	31	33	N	Cold
26	28	49	38	35	37	N	Mild
27	28	54	47	40	42	N	Clear and warm
28	37	60	55	47	49	E	Clear
29	46	65	69	55	56	W	Clear
30	42	67	61	58	58	E	Clear

SANITARY REPORT.

Barometrical Table—Highest at Morning, Noon and Evening.

D.of M.	JANUARY, 1860. A.M.	M.	P.M.	M.M.	D.of M.	FEBRUARY, 1860. A.M.	M.	P.M.	M.H.	D.of M.	MARCH, 1860. A.M.	M.	P.M.	M.H.	D.of M.	APRIL, 1860. A.M.	M.	P.M.	M.M.
1	29 30	29 30	29 50	29 45	1	29 34	29 51	29 50	29 45	1	29 06	29 06	29 20	29 11	1	28 76	28 74	28 66	28 72
2	29 52	29 50	29 50	29 51	2	29 30	29 30	29 60	29 53	2	29 30	29 30	29 40	29 33	2	28 77	28 82	28 81	28 82
3	29 50	29 50	29 45	29 47	3	29 53	29 45	29 38	29 45	3	29 23	29 19	29 03	29 15	3	28 82	28 83	28 74	28 77
4	29 50	29 45	29 65	29 62	4	29 40	29 45	29 44	29 44	4	29 24	29 24	29 24	29 24	4	28 72	28 69	28 55	28 65
5	29 55	29 65	29 50	29 57	5	29 41	29 47	29 11	29 31	5	29 10	29 00	29 00	29 03	5	28 72	28 73	28 70	28 71
6	29 55	29 60	29 10	29 17	6	29 00	29 99	29 98	28 99	6	29 00	29 08	29 98	29 02	6	28 92	29 01	28 82	28 94
7	29 30	29 10	29 10	29 15	7	29 03	29 19	29 24	29 15	7	28 85	28 86	28 88	28 86	7	29 02	29 07	29 06	29 05
8	29 20	29 25	29 25	29 18	8	29 22	29 18	29 14	29 18	8	29 00	29 98	29 94	28 97	8	29 06	29 04	29 05	29 05
9	29 30	29 30	29 30	29 30	9	29 03	29 91	29 93	29 96	9	28 90	28 99	29 90	28 89	9	29 02	29 04	29 03	29 03
10	29 30	29 30	29 36	29 29	10	29 30	29 29	29 40	29 33	10	28 90	28 00	29 10	29 00	10	29 03	29 00	29 04	29 03
11	29 14	29 10	29 14	29 21	11	29 13	29 93	29 98	29 01	11	29 13	29 14	29 00	29 09	11	29 03	29 02	29 09	29 04
12	29 52	29 38	29 12	29 31	12	29 32	29 36	29 44	29 32	12	28 70	28 88	29 10	28 89	12	29 19	29 19	29 19	29 19
13	29 40	29 43	29 42	29 45	13	29 25	29 18	29 10	29 18	13	29 22	29 22	29 22	29 22	13	29 18	29 14	29 14	29 18
14	29 23	29 05	28 88	29 05	14	29 12	29 15	29 13	29 14	14	29 22	29 22	29 24	29 32	14	29 16	29 16	29 16	29 16
15	28 94	28 94	28 97	28 95	15	28 97	28 85	28 88	28 89	15	28 28	28 33	28 36	28 36	15	29 21	29 22	29 20	29 20
16	28 97	28 98	28 98	28 98	16	28 91	28 96	29 02	28 96	16	29 36	29 36	29 36	29 36	16	29 23	29 25	29 25	29 24
17	28 98	28 98	28 98	28 98	17	29 10	29 10	29 10	29 03	17	29 36	29 36	29 35	29 37	17	20 02	29 09	29 32	29 14
18	28 98	29 98	29 99	28 98	18	28 42	29 21	29 49	29 38	18	29 40	29 38	29 38	29 38	18	29 40	29 49	29 45	29 43
19	29 13	29 15	29 15	29 15	19	28 90	29 04	29 20	29 03	19	29 00	29 00	29 15	29 17	19	29 43	29 48	29 40	29 43
20	29 20	29 20	29 20	29 21	20	29 18	29 18	29 18	29 29	20	29 00	29 00	29 00	29 00	20	29 22	29 25	29 29	29 22	
21	29 18	29 18	29 18	29 21	21	29 21	29 21	29 26	29 29	21	29 03	29 03	29 03	29 04	21	29 19	29 04	29 04	29 07	
22	29 18	29 19	29 22	29 20	22	29 91	29 88	29 80	28 86	22	29 05	29 07	29 00	29 06	22	29 00	29 02	29 01	29 01	
23	29 37	29 49	29 49	29 42	23	28 80	29 01	29 83	28 88	23	29 06	29 03	29 87	29 99	23	20 00	29 03	29 00	29 03	
24	29 38	29 36	29 20	29 33	24	29 02	29 06	29 28	29 04	24	28 98	28 87	29 86	29 87						
25	29 28	28 29	29 35	29 31	25	29 12	29 34	29 30	29 23	25	28 86	28 86	29 86	29 86						
26	29 25	29 25	29 03	29 21	26	29 50	29 41	29 44	29 47	26	28 86	28 86	29 06	29 01						
27	29 19	29 19	29 20	29 19	27	29 41	29 44	29 50	29 43	27	29 13	29 13	29 13	29 13						
28	28 91	29 92	29 30	29 07	28	29 44	29 50	29 38	29 48	28	29 03	29 03	29 06	29 05						
29	29 30	29 25	29 10	29 22	29	29 40	29 23	29 36	29 33	29	29 00	29 04	29 85	29 95						
30	29 07	29 09	29 14	29 10						30	29 92	29 83	29 93	29 93						
31	29 17	29 17	29 22	29 19						31	29 92	29 92	29 80	29 88						

Mortality.—The absence of a registration law prevents us from reporting the mortality of the diseases met with in this county. I am not aware that any mortuary tables have been kept by any physician in the county.

The following will approximate very closely to the mortality of the different diseases:—

In Typhoid fever	1 in 15 cases.
" Remittent "	1 in 40 "
" Smallpox	1 in 20 "
" Varioloid	none.
" Measles	1 in 50 "
" Pneumonia	1 in 20 "
" Pleurisy	1 in 20 "

In different forms of nervous diseases, 1 in 50; in different forms of disease of organs of nutrition, 1 in 15; in diseases of urino-genital organs, 1 in 8.

Prevalent Diseases.—Our county has been remarkably exempt from epidemics and endemics during the past year. Scarlatina, Rubeola and Pertussis were met with in a few localities; but, most cases were mild.

Fevers.—*Intermittent Fever* is rarely met with. Sometimes a few cases occur which have been contracted abroad. They generally yield to appropriate treatment.

Remittent Fever has been more prevalent than in former years; it is mostly confined to a few localities. Some cases are severe, and occasionally fatal; but few are troublesome when promptly treated.

Typhus Fever is not met with.

Typhoid Fever is a common disease in this county; it prevails, more or less every year, commencing generally in the early part of summer, and continues during the fall, and sometimes into the winter. It is not considered contagious, nor is it very fatal. I have observed the first cases in the season to commence on the east side of streams, and occasionally where there was but a small quantity of pure fresh water, but moisture, more or less, on the west side of the residences. In a few localities in the county, contiguous to mill-dams and other ponds of water, it frequently assumes remissions simulating remittent fever.

At Greenville and Dimondsville this form prevailed, and many of the cases were fatal. Dr. W. B. Stewart of Greenville, informs me that during an epidemic in that place, in the best marked cases of typhoid, with all the general and local symptoms of the disease, a few doses of sulphate of quinine would give it a remittent form.

The treatment pursued by most physicians in the county is such as is laid down in the text books.

I have administered quin. sulp. in small doses (one grain) about every three or four hours, in connection with such remedies as are required to control the local and general disturbances with the happiest effects. I frequently commence the quinine at my first visit, and have never seen cause to regret it. I believe quinine has very much the same specific influence on the peculiar poison in the blood of a typhoid patient, that it has in intermittent and remittent diseases. I think the great error of many is in the administration of large doses;—large doses never succeeded well in my practice. The doses should be small and well-timed, so that it will be taken up in the circulation without making a strong impression on the nervous system. Since I adopted this course of treatment, in good constitutions, without any complication, I seldom lose a case, or have erysipelas or abscess in the last stage of the disease.

In May, 1858, there were a few cases of typhoid fever on a branch of the Mahoning Creek, that assumed a very malignant form. About a week from the commencement of the attack, on some part of the surface a severe burning sensation would be felt, very painful to the touch; in a few hours it would become red, then purple, and shortly after, black; generally, not more than twelve hours from the time the pain was first felt, the part would begin to slough, and even the bones would exfoliate. most of the cases died. A great many remedies were tried; but the treatment that appeared to mitigate the symptoms most was quinia and spirits turpentine, pushed as far as the patients would bear, with anodynes sufficient to allay pain and procure rest. Some of them lived until portions of the body sloughed and dropped off.

It may be proper to remark here that no mercurial was used in any of the cases.

Smallpox is not often met with. Sometimes vaccination is neglected for a year or two, and a few cases may be contracted before it can be accomplished for protection. The members of the profession generally concur in attesting the value and power of vaccination.

Measles.—There are generally cases of measles every year; they are but seldom fatal, unless there is some complication. The antiphlogistic treatment is sometimes necessary; but, generally, an expectant one is all that is required.

Scarlatina.—Almost every year it is seen, but not generally of a virulent character. It has prevailed epidemically every six or seven years, when it is more malignant, and frequently very fatal. No disease has been treated in a greater variety of forms than this. Some have tried the stimulating plan of treatment, by administering alcoholic preparations throughout the course of the disease; but I believe this mode of treatment has but few advocates in this part of the country at present. Most practitioners pursue a cautious antiphlogistic treatment. The veratrum viride has been extolled by some. Others depend on cold ablutions; while others again prefer to treat with chloride of potassa. Chloride of sodium, in solution with capsicum, is frequently used for a gargle.

OTHER DISEASES.—*Pneumonia* occurs in all parts of the county during the winter and spring; it is generally of a sthenic character. Active antiphlogistic treatment is required in most cases. But one communication has been received on this disease. Dr. Anthony, of Marion, writes: "In November and December I had a number of cases of pneumonia, all of whom recovered. The treatment in all the cases was phlebotomy, cupping, antimony and morphia, to act as a sedative and expectorant; and in some, mercurials were pushed till the gums were slightly affected. Also, counter-irritation, with blisters six by eight inches."

Pleurisy is very common in this part of the country. It generally yields to prompt antiphlogistic treatment.

Heart Diseases.—During the past year there were more heart affections than has been known before. Many of them proved fatal. Some very suddenly. There was one peculiarity about most of the cases—a large number of them were among those in comfortable circumstances; that lived well, the most industrious, and generally of regular and temperate habits.

Inflammatory Rheumatism is very common in our county. It appears to be on the increase; it is not generally manageable by the treatment recommended in most of the text books. Many physicians have varied their mode of treatment in this disease very much. I have not been favored with any communications on this subject.

From what intercourse I have had with other members of the profession, I learn that many depend much on iodide of potassium after the acute inflammatory period is passed. I have used, sometimes with decided benefit, something like the following: "Bichloride of mercury 10 or 12 grains, muriate of ammonia 1 drachm, iodide of potassium 1½ ozs., water 1 pint; dose from 40 to 60 drops three or four times a day."

Within the last few months I treated a few cases with tartrate of soda and potassa and veratrum viride, with anodynes at night sufficient to procure rest and allay pain. I am free to say that I never had rheumatic cases to do as well as those under this mode of treatment.

Consumption has been increasing rapidly during the last few years; it forms a very large space in the mortuary list of our county. Most cases are hereditary, a few can be traced to neglected colds, &c.; but the gradual increased hereditary tendency is truly alarming to the sanitary observer. It is not necessary to speak of the treatment or the result of the treatment, it is here the same as in all other places.

Scrofula is frequently met with; a large portion of the cases are hereditary, and generally terminate in phthisis.

MISCELLANEOUS.—*Veratrum Viride* may properly be considered a new remedy amongst our physicians, and has generally been satisfactory; in many cases it is spoken of in the highest terms as to its controlling influences over the heart and arteries. As far as I have tried it I have been pleased with its effects; when used for a length of time, diarrhœa generally sets in.

Yellow Jessamine (Gelseminum sempervirens) has been tried in gonorrhœa, without producing any decided change.

The *Hypophosphates* have been tried by a few physicians without giving satisfaction.

Surgery.—The surgical cases during the past year have not been numerous, occasionally an amputation; a few cases of the extirpation of the mammary glands, with fractures of the extremities and clavicle are the principal. In fractures of the femur, Dessault's apparatus is generally used.

In fractures of the leg, the fracture box is used by some, others prefer a modification of Dessault's apparatus. In fractures of the clavicle, Fox's apparatus with a shoulder-brace.

May 4th, I was called to see a boy aged 6 years and 1 month; he had received the contents of a double-barrelled shotgun loaded with buckshot, over the left eye, sweeping away part of the frontal, and a greater part of the temporal bone, with integument and part of the brain, back as far as the ear; some particles of brain were carried through a tin vessel several feet from the boy. He lived 23 hours; he appeared unconscious nearly all the time; never spoke; sometimes moaned like a person in sleep.

OBSTETRICAL.—Of 404 births reported, 214 were males, and 190 females; no communications furnished by the members of society.

April 30, 1860, I was called to attend Mrs. I., æt. 36, her fifth pregnancy. She informed me that she had had symptoms of labor for more than two weeks, had been wasting a great deal during that time, and the last ten days compelled to keep her bed all the time on account of the loss of blood, whenever she would move or get up. At this time she was very weak. I made an examination and felt the placenta through the os uteri, which was dilated about an inch in diameter. I administered a large dose of ergot, and immediately after, carefully introduced my hand into the vagina, passing my fingers gradually into the os uteri. About the time I was able to pass my hand into the womb her pains commenced to bear down, I separated the placenta on one side by sweeping the fingers along the inner surface of the organ, passing up the hand as soon as possible, brought down a foot, and with the aid of the bearing down pains she was delivered of the child in a short time. I discovered she was wasting profusely, the placenta was torn across. I immediately introduced my hand and removed the part that was remaining in the womb; this being done, the womb contracted well; she was very much prostrated; the pillows were removed, the foot of the bed elevated from eight to ten inches, and by the administration of mild restoratives she soon rallied, and mother and child are doing well.

January 30, 1860, Mrs. M., aged 19, felt very unwell with pain in her stomach; by advice of a lady friend, took camphor and laudanum for the pain; was about eight months advanced in her second pregnancy; she had a miscarriage of four months' advance, 24th of February, 1859; her husband was absent from home, and no one to stay with her but a young girl. She retired about her usual time, the girl in another part of the house; next morning when the girl had breakfast ready, she went to her room and found her in convulsions. I was called in, bled her very largely, applied ice and snow to her head, ordered mustard and friction to the lower extremities, cupped her freely along the spine, applied a blister to the nape of the neck, endeavored to get her to swallow, but failed; the convulsions continued every half hour until between 4 and 5 o'clock P. M. About 2 o'clock the os uteri commenced to dilate, and continued dilating slowly, and with the struggling and convulsive efforts the head descended far enough at 4 o'clock in the afternoon to be reached by the forceps, which I applied and delivered her, the placenta soon following; the convulsions now ceased, she swallowed a little wine and water, never spoke, lay in a comatose condition till 8 o'clock P. M., when she expired.

There were two women delivered in the county, where the placenta was full of chalky concretions; the uterine surface of one of them was very rough.

Dr. Anthony reports a case as follows: "I attended a lady at her confinement; the child's health was good until the third day, when it gave evidence of being unwell; the nurse observed a red spot on the centre of the occipital region about the size of a dime. I was called in that evening. When I reached the place, the inflammation and swelling had extended over all the occipital region, and partly over the top of the head. The red spot which was observed first had become gangrenous, and the following morning sloughed and separated from the adjacent tissues, leaving the cranium exposed about three-fourths of an inch in diameter. The superficial fascia sloughed out about the size of a dollar. The opening in the skin enlarged but little more than the fascia. The discharge from the surface was very offensive.

I gave laxatives sufficient to insure an evacuation from the bowels daily, also iodide potassa 1-5 grain four times a day. Applied to the slough a decoction of black oak bark three times a day, and over the inflamed surface unguent. plumb. acetas three times a day, with a poultice of bread and milk coated over with the mucilage of slippery elm over all the affected surface, renewed frequently. The sloughing of the superficial fascia ceased in two or three days, and the child gradually convalesced.

The space left by the slough gradually healed over. The child at present appears healthy."

Tobacco.—Most persons are satisfied that many of the hereditary diseases are increasing among us, with fearful rapidity. We cannot help pausing at times, and ask ourselves the question, Why is this so? What is the cause or causes of this change in the human family? No one will doubt that there are many causes for it; but, by examining one by one, the supposed or real causes, carefully and impartially, we must say that the excessive use of tobacco, so common in our country for many years past, is the principal. No article so injurious to the human economy is in so general use—we might say universal use. The habit is so common, that persons not addicted to it might be termed exceptions. Wood & Bache, in the United States Dispensatory, speaking of the effects of tobacco, say, that "Tobacco, when used in excess, enfeebles digestion, produces emaciation, and general debility; and lays the foundation of serious nervous disorders—sometimes mental disorder, closely resembling delirium tremens." It is liable to disorder the digestive organs, and produce general debility. Can the blood be in a healthy state during the use of an accumulative toxic principle? I think not. If the blood is not affected, why the emaciation and serious nervous derangement? Is not the blood the source from which the component parts of every tissue derives its material? The modification of its elements must then modify the secretory—the nutrient, as well as the nervous action.

Are not hereditary diseases produced by some primary modification in the constitution or elements of the blood? It is well known that this agent will affect the system, applied locally, taken into the mouth, or inhaled into the lungs. It has proved fatal in many cases, administered in different forms. In all the defects and changes in the blood, each particle must participate, and the solids suffer in proportion to their physiological relation; hence the corresponding changes in the secretions.

The nervous derangement is another evidence of its destructive property, as the nervous system is subject to influences through the blood, and is deeply implicated in all the phenomena of the living being, in health and disease.

I think it will not be disputed that the system of the tobacco chewer and smoker becomes saturated with the substance; for instance, subject one of them to a process, like what the hydropathist calls packing, and then examine the linen. I need not offer more.

Now, the main question may be put: Can an unhealthy being, diseased, poisoned, and emaciated, beget the reverse? We all know that there are certain tendencies and predispositions; and these are generally inherited. Will not everything that impairs health and depresses the vital organism favor the natural tendency? We have the law that the "parents eat sour grapes, and the children's teeth are set on edge." We have no evidence that the persons eating the grapes suffered like the children.

We may venture one step farther. Is not this habit the foundation of drunkenness in our land? By an impartial investigation, we not only find disease produced, but morbid appetites. It is not often that we see a person fond of strong drink, that is not a slave to tobacco in some form. In most of our villages and towns, we see boys from seven to ten years of age, chewing and smoking. If we watch their course, the majority of them will be drunkards at twenty-five.

Many are of opinion that it is the tasting of intoxicating drinks that makes the drunkard; close investigation will not sustain this opinion. Many years ago these western counties were studded with small distilleries, and the young men that were raised up about them are among the most temperate in their neighborhood; many of them not tasting a drop. Occasionally you will meet with one addicted to strong drink; in these instances you generally find that they spent much time in idleness, and used tobacco in some form; and had companions with the same habits.

I have neither time nor ability to do justice to this subject, nor in a report of this kind is it expected; but I wished to notice it merely, that the subject may be taken up by those who are able to do justice to one of so much magnitude.

It is with regret that a report so unsatisfactory is submitted; but, circumstances prevent anything better at this time.

It was late in the season when the committee was appointed, and unfortunately, I have had no opportunity of meeting the other members of the committee, for the purpose of preparing a report; and received only two communications, one on Pneumonia, and the other on Infantile Erysipelas. The work was delayed to the latest period, and I have been compelled to report what I am in possession of, aware that it presents little worthy of consideration. Respectfully submitted,

WM. ANDERSON.

REPORT OF THE INDIANA COUNTY MEDICAL SOCIETY.

The locality, hydrography, topography, and geology of our county were given in the report of 1860.

Meteorology and Mortality no data—As the county lies between the Appalachian chain of mountains and the Lakes, we are subjected to frequent, sudden, and severe changes of weather. During the winter months, we have seldom a week of settled weather at any one time. Most generally, there occurs a change of the atmosphere every twenty-four hours, during that season. Our people are very subject to severe colds, and most of our prevalent diseases during the winter have an inflammatory tendency.

During the summer of 1863, we had no fall of rain between May and November; there was, in consequence, a great scarcity of water during the fall and early part of winter. In our towns and villages, the water of many wells became offensive and unfit for use. In these localities we had a large number of cases of Remittent Fever. Many cases were severe and protracted, the patients generally complained of pain or uneasiness in the stomach, loss of appetite, headache, and general languor for several days before they were compelled to go to bed. These symptoms were followed by chills, alternating with flushes of heat; nausea, frequently vomiting; severe pain in the head; pain in the back and loins; soreness over the entire body, attended with muscular weakness.

In the larger number of cases, there were two remissions every twenty-four hours, in the fore part of the day, and fore part of the night. The pulse at first was full, but soon became more slow and feeble. The gastric disturbance continued throughout the disease. After the first week, many of the cases exhibited a typhoid tendency, with pain in the back, more particularly at the cervical and dorsal regions. The duration of the attack was usually from two to four weeks.

Treatment.—In a few cases venesection was required. An emetic of ipecac. gave great relief in most cases. This was followed by calomel, rhubarb and ginger, sufficient to move the bowels freely; then calomel, opium, and ipecac., in alterative doses, until a slight mercurial impression was produced. After this, small doses of quiniæ sulphas and chlorate of potassa were found to be valuable remedies. A dose of Dover's powder was given at night, when the stomach would bear it; in other cases, the sulphate of morphia, opium, or laudanum. Sinapisms were applied along the spine and over the stomach. Cold applications were made to the head, and warm applications to the extremities. Where the pain was constant and severe in the head and back, blisters were invaluable remedies.

Abscesses were very common in the last stages of the disease; most generally on the back and about the neck.

When the pulse continued frequent, veratrum viride was found to be useful. Most of the cases recovered.

Rheumatism has been more frequently met with last year

than formerly; the acute inflammatory form was the most common; all ages were attacked, and almost all the cases ran a protracted course.

Treatment.—The iodide of potassium, chlorate of potassa, bicarbonate of soda, citrate of potassa, Rochelle salts, guaiacum and colchicum, have all been tried. The course of treatment found most beneficial in my practice was, evacuating the bowels freely at the commencement of the attack with calomel, podophyllin, and extract colocynth; then the administration of calomel, opium and ipecac., in alterative doses, until a slight mercurial impression was apparent. This was followed by bicarbonate of soda, or Rochelle salt, in full doses, every three or four hours.

Dover's powder, or morphia sulphas, sufficient to allay pain, was given, and the veratrum viride to control the heart's action.

In obstinate cases, the following preparation has had good effect:—

>Bichloride of mercury, 10 grains,
>Muriate of ammonia, 1 drachm,
>Iodide of potassium, 1½ oz.
>To be dissolved in a pint of water.

Dose, from 30 to 60 drops 3 times a day, in hop-tea or sweetened water.

Cupping the spine was found beneficial in some cases. Bleeding and blistering were not esteemed advisable, unless the disease assumed an irregular form.

Pneumonia prevailed more generally last winter than was ever known to be the case before in our county. All ages were attacked; persons advanced in life were mostly affected with regular pneumonia, and the middle aged and young, with broncho and pleuro-pneumonia. At first there were generally chills, a flushed face and headache, with some fever; hurried respiration; a feeling of weight or oppression in the chest; constipation; in many of the cases there was very little thirst. The duration of the disease was from eight to twelve days. If the case became protracted, cerebral disturbance would often occur.

Treatment.—The majority of our physicians treated the discase by venesection, purgatives, expectorants, cupping and blistering. But more cases have been treated lately without the lancet than formerly; the veratrum viride being chiefly depended on to control the action of the heart. Mercury to affect the system; antimonials and blisters.

The course I found most successful in the cases that came under my care was—if my patient was an adult and plethoric—to bleed, then purge, mostly with calomel, followed with black draught. After this I gave alterative doses of calomel, opium, ipecac., and digitalis, every three hours till the gums were affected; Dover's powder or morphia at night, to procure rest; blistered freely. If this course did not control the fever, I used veratrum viride to keep the pulse natural. I gave my patients tartar emetic and morphia in solution, for the cough; two parts of the former to one of the latter, regulated according to age and condition, every one, two, or three hours.

Venesection in robust, plethoric persons, will cut short the disease several days.

Measles.—During the last two years, we have had severe epidemics of this disease; it affected persons of all ages, from infancy to sixty years. The symptoms, at the commencement of the attack, were feeble pulse, difficulty in breathing, oppression at the epigastric region. In some cases there were delirium and other nervous disturbances, with a strong tendency to inflammation of the lungs, and sometimes of the stomach and the brain; severe pain in the head and back, with continued vomiting, was also observed. In the most severe cases the eruption did not appear until the fifth or sixth day. It was mostly irregular and of a livid hue. Many of the cases proved fatal.

Treatment.—The most successful treatment was by calomel, opium, and ipecac., in alterative doses, followed by full doses of chlorate of potassa, with tepid drinks, low diet, laxatives, veratrum to allay fever; tartrate of antimony and morphia in solution to allay cough and difficulty of breathing; opium and acetate of lead in cases attended with diarrhœa. After the disappearance of the eruption, if any congestion or inflammation remained, local depletion and blisters, with the cautious use of stimulants and tonics, were necessary.

Scarlatina prevailed in many parts of the county last year; most of the cases commenced with sickness of stomach, vomiting, sore throat, fever, and quick pulse. The disease was of a favorable type. In some families, during last winter, scarlatina and measles prevailed at the same time, or, as soon as the one had run its course, the other commencing.

Treatment.—Laxatives, chlorate of potassa internally; tepid drinks; veratrum to allay fever; cold applications to the head; sinapisms to the spine; opium and acetate of lead to arrest diarrhœa; tartar emetic and morphia in solution to allay bronchial or pulmonary disturbance. Sponging the surface with tepid water and soap was found to be very soothing to the patient.

Diphtheria has prevailed in our county for the last four years, in all localities, town and country, low and elevated, dry and moist, and during both summer and winter. The mortality has been the same, or nearly so, in every locality. Sometimes the disease would assume a mild form for a few weeks, almost every case terminating favorably, then it would become more fatal. In general, new cases were observed to appear about two days after heavy rains, during the winter season. In cases where there was much swelling of the glands of the neck, with rapid formation of deposit on the tonsils and uvula, the disease was of a grave form; few cases recovered when the deposit extended to the larynx—I believe only two in my practice. In such cases death seemed to be gradually approaching for some thirty-six hours before the deposit became detached and thrown off. I had many cases where the deposit was thrown off, but soon re-formed, and the patients sank. I found that many of the cases in which emetics and purgatives produced little effect, and where there was a refusal to partake of a reasonable amount of nourishment, proved fatal. My opinion is, that diphtheria is a blood disease, non-contagious, and distinct from all others, though, perhaps, closely allied to scarlatina; the sequelæ of the two diseases are, however, very different. In diphtheria the tendency is to paralysis; in scarlatina to dropsy and abscess. Scarlatina is seldom met with more than once in the same individual. In diphtheria, frequently several attacks may occur in the same individual. I have had persons under my care that had had four attacks within twelve months. Occasionally scarlatina and diphtheria prevailed in the same families, when one run its course, the other commencing.

Treatment.—It is very seldom that we meet with as much difference of sentiment in respect to treatment as we do in this disease. After many trials the treatment that has been found most successful in our county, as far as I can ascertain, consists in the application of soothing remedies to the throat, and the administration internally of such as are adapted to change the condition of the blood as quickly as possible.

Local Treatment.—Warm poultices to the neck, if there is much swelling. A poultice of hops and vinegar, thickened with bran, applied warm and frequently changed, was found beneficial. The fatty portion of old bacon, sliced thin and applied around the neck, was also esteemed a good application, as was also the camphor liniment. A gargle of vinegar, pepper, and salt, used every hour or two, as strong as the patient can bear it, is one of the best remedies I ever tried. Where there is much tenderness in the throat a strong decoction of the *quercus alba* will be found useful. In some cases the camphor liniment is soothing to the tonsils.

General Treatment.—An active purgative at first, followed by full doses of chlorate of potassa in solution, every three or four hours, throughout the course of the disease, with a moderately good diet, such as the patient can swallow. In cases of great debility, hot toddy or other alcoholic stimulant, to be taken warm and administered liberally.

Emetics should always be at hand. Should there be any

tightness about the throat or chest, an emetic should be administered immediately. I prefer ipecac., or ipecac. and alum mixed. If fever should be present after an active purgative, veratrum viride should be used to control the morbid action of the heart.

Chlorate of potassa given alone has been more beneficial as an internal remedy in this disease than any other I have tried. Iodide of potassium has proved beneficial in some cases, but disturbed the stomach in many others, keeping up nausea, with loss of appetite. Muriated tincture of iron had a great reputation at one time—both administered internally and applied to the tonsils. It was very frequently added to a saturated solution of chlorate of potassa; but I have failed to see any decided benefit from it in this disease, though prescribed in over two hundred cases. Quiniæ sulphas has been frequently tried; but few cases have been benefited by it. Where it disagreed with the patient, as it did in very many cases, it produced spasmodic disturbance, and in a few cases convulsions. The same effects resulted from Peruvian bark and Fowler's solution. Veratrum viride is useful in allaying excitement of the arterial system; but I never saw any other good effect from its use in this disease. Mercury has proved useful in a few cases where there was a strong tendency to inflammation, but not in others. Guaiacum and colchicum have little or no influence over the disease. Alum was useful in a few cases where there was profuse hemorrhage from the nose, internally administered. Blisters to the neck, or in the vicinity of the neck, are positively injurious. I am free to say that injury was inflicted upon every patient I blistered in diphtheria. It had the effect to increase the extent of the disease in the very part which it is so important to protect. Croton oil and all irritants to the neck proved injurious, just in proportion to their strength. Tincture of iodine has been used by many physicians, applied to the cervical glands and to the tonsils with a brush; but it is now pretty generally abandoned as useless, if not injurious. In the hands of our physicians, hydrochloric acid diluted has been tried, but has failed to give satisfaction. I have given the nitrate of silver frequent and fair trials, both in the form of pencil and in solution, and never saw any benefit from its use; but believe it was injurious in many cases. Swabbing the throat and forcibly detaching the deposit is highly injurious. Everything irritating to the throat should be avoided. Such is my experience in at least six hundred cases. The mortality in my practice was as follows: In the year 1860, 1 in 43; 1861, 1 in 10; 1862, 1 in 15; 1863, 1 in 20.

Cerebro-Spinal Meningitis.—We have had a number of cases of this form of disease within the last eighteen months in our county. It commenced in two forms—in the greater number of cases without any premonitory symptoms. The patient was suddenly attacked with pain in the head and vomiting. Some had a strong desire for food immediately before vomiting commenced. There soon followed pain in the back, difficulty in breathing, distressed appearance of the countenance, and delirium. In the majority of cases the pulse was small and frequent at first; in others it was not much changed.

In severe attacks the surface is generally cold at first. Delirium commences early, with agitation of the muscles, followed by moaning. The eyes are generally affected; sometimes the pupil is contracted; in others dilated. There is often inflammation of the eyes, with intolerance of light, as well as of sound. In a few cases there is insensibility to light, with deafness. There is great thirst, constipation, and suspension of the secretions generally. Early in the disease the muscles of the neck become contracted, drawing the head mostly backwards; in other cases a little to one side. Occasionally the spinal muscles are rigid, even to the lower extremities. Many attacked in this way die in from twelve to thirty-six hours.

In the other form of attack the patient complains for several days of lightness of head, weakness, loss of appetite, general soreness of the body, with occasional sharp pain at some particular part. Occasionally symptoms of pneumonia or pleurisy present themselves for a few hours; then there takes place a sudden transition of symptoms to the bowels, peritoneum, kidneys, or brain. The disturbance may continue in this way for several days, often deceiving superficial observers as to the true seat of disease, until the period when relief may be rendered has passed.

In this form the symptoms are generally periodical. When suffering, the patient has a wild, vacant stare, and answers questions incoherently, most generally saying he is much better, and thinks he will be well soon. Pressure along the spine will lead to tender spots, of which the patient was not before conscious. After a few days of periodical and shifting disturbance the patient presents a distressed and delirious aspect, stupor gradually becoming more and more intense. There is generally moaning, with restlessness. The lightest touch will frequently cause complaint. If this comatose condition lasts long the patient is sure to die.

Relapses are generally fatal. All ages are liable to be attacked. I have seen it in persons two years old, and of all ages up to seventy. Both sexes are liable; but the larger number attacked are females, between sixteen and twenty-five years of age, and unmarried. I never saw a married lady suffering from the disease. Abscess is occasionally met with in the advanced stages of the disease; but it is not of frequent occurrence. In some cases petechiæ and rose-colored spots make their appearance.

Recovery is very slow, even when the stomach will bear a good deal of nourishment, and the bowels are at the same time regular. The patient becomes more and more emaciated, until he becomes wasted to the condition of a living skeleton. In these cases the appearance of the face is deceptive. I have seen the face full and the features natural when the patient was on the verge of dissolution. I supposed this disparity between the condition of the features and of the frame to result from the seat of the disease, in consequence of which the important line of communication between the brain and the digestive organs is interrupted, the recuperative powers of the system being thereby impaired or destroyed.

Treatment.—Few diseases require more active treatment. If the patient is robust, I bleed freely at first. After venesection, if performed early in the attack, the pulse frequently becomes more full. Large doses of calomel, followed by black draught, should then be given until the bowels are freely moved; then alterative doses of calomel, opium, ipecac. and digitalis, until the gums are affected. The hair should be thinned, and cold applications made to the head, with blisters to the nape of the neck. Sinapisms along the spine, over the stomach, and to the lower extremities. If fever supervenes, veratrum viride will be proper in sufficient doses to keep the pulse regular. After the mercurial has made an impression on the system, iodide of potassium is the best remedy that I have tried.

I believe blisters will prove the most useful agent in this disease, if commenced with early and followed up. When I commence to blister in this disease I put the first on the nape of the neck, and as soon as it commences to dry I put another on between the shoulders; when it commences to dry I put another again on the nape of the neck, and so change them alternately throughout the course of the disease.

I have used chlorate of potassa after a mercurial impression is made; but believe it is not of much account in bad cases. Quiniæ sulphas I believe is injurious. I have tried it, and have seen other cases where it was used, and it seemed to me to produce disturbance in nearly all the cases in which it was tried. I have used Fowler's solution, and arsenious acid and iron in the advanced stages of the disease. Neither of these remedies was beneficial; but their effects were most generally injurious. Opiates usually agree well with the patients, and are useful in procuring rest. I have found that those patients did the best who were kept calm by means of opiates.

Attention should be paid to the patient's skin and secretions generally, throughout the whole course of treatment. Some amount of nourishment ought to be insisted upon after three or four days, and if symptoms of debility approach rapidly, diffusible stimulants used cautiously will be indispensable.

In 1865 Dr. Anderson was elected president of the Medical Society of the State of Pennsylvania, and was conducted to the chair by Drs. King, of Pittsburg, and Zeigler, of Lancaster. On taking chair he made the following remarks:

GENTLEMEN:—I tender you my thanks for the partiality you have shown in selecting me to preside over the deliberations of this Society, among whose members so many are my superiors in medical knowledge as well as in parliamentary experience. I cannot think that this honor is to me alone, but also to the Society I represent.

Since I first held a seat in the State Society, I have felt a deep interest in its success, and have endeavored, to the extent of my ability, to promote the great object of its organization. It is true, the profession throughout the State have not responded to the frequent appeals made to them by this Society in the manner that many of us desired. But we should not despair. There is certainly a brighter day approaching. We are firmly of opinion that much of the opposition and influence against us from irregular practitioners and quacks must soon yield. Had it not been for our domestic difficulties during the last four years, I believe much of our desired work would have been done ere this. But view our situation, weigh our surroundings, take into careful consideration the great struggle that has been going on to preserve the life of our nation, and see how it has affected every district, and family, I might say, in our land. The physician, whose mission it is to go about doing good, has performed his full share in the camp, in the field, and at home. These duties resting on him unavoidably, will account for what some might construe as indifference. Our profession, as well as the enlightened portion of every community, have learned by fearful experience the consequences of tolerating an institution in direct opposition to light and knowledge. We should profit by the fearful lesson we have had, and take advantage of the educated sentiment in the masses of mankind, with renewed assurances that the worthy objects of our noble profession shall not fail. Knowing well that quackery soon begins to reel and stagger in the presence of well-regulated medical organizations, it behooves every member of our State and local societies in the commonwealth to be alive to the work of organization, until our annual meetings will be composed of delegates from every county and city of the glorious old Keystone, making her truly the keystone of medical science as well as she is of our republican institutions.

Gentlemen, I again thank you for the honor conferred upon me, and ask your aid and indulgence in the performance of the duties of my official station.

ADDRESS OF THE PRESIDENT,
WM. ANDERSON, M. D.

Gentlemen of the Medical Society of the State of Pennsylvania:

In obedience to the Constitution I come before you to fulfil a duty required of the presiding officer, and, in performing the duty assigned me, I am at a loss to find language adequate to express the happiness I feel in renewing with many of you the pleasant associations of former years, and of greeting those who are present for the first time, to promote our honorable interests, and to contribute their well-earned knowledge for the benefit of our profession and the good of mankind.

With the return of another (the seventeenth) anniversary of the Medical Society of the State of Pennsylvania, we cannot but experience some feelings of regret that the profession has not been sufficiently awake to the importance of a thorough medical organization throughout our State: especially when we view the delegates in attendance, and find so many counties in the State are without medical organizations, and consequently without representation. But the consciousness of doing good and of belonging to that brotherhood of science which has achieved so much for humanity, and is destined to achieve still more, and a desire to be co-workers in the great study of nature and man, have brought a goodly number here to-day. These annual meetings may relieve us for a short period from the active labors of professional life; but they cannot relieve us from the responsibility of our calling, which inspires to higher and nobler thoughts than the outbursts of popular pleasure; and all of us who have the privilege of mutually congratulating each other on this occasion, should determine anew, individually and collectively, to do our duty, so as to make ourselves more useful, to elevate the profession, and advance the science of medicine. Every physician should recollect the obligation he is under to his profession. It is not sufficient that he appropriates all the wisdom and learning accumulated by medical organization, and disseminated by publication, to himself, but it is his imperative duty to give to others the result of his wisdom and experience. This mental attrition sharpens the faculties, and cultivates a spirit of investigation, which is a feature of medical organization. We should also bear in mind that, within the borders of Pennsylvania, the first regular medical school was established on this continent, and from that day to the present the students of her medical colleges have been respectable in numbers, as well as in character; and wherever met are considered worthy members of their honorable and honored class.

In consideration that the interests of the profession, the increase of medical science, in this age of discoveries in physiology, chemistry, meteria medica, surgery, and the practice of medicine, could be better promoted by well-regulated medical organizations; a respectable number of the profession met, eighteen years ago, and formed our present Society, and declared the following basis to be its object.

"The objects of this Society shall be the advancement of medical knowledge, the elevation of professional character, the protection of the interests of its members, the extension of the bounds of medical science, and the promotion of all measures adapted to the relief of suffering, and to improve the health and protect the lives of the community."

These objects and principles appeal at once to the best interests of every regular member of the profession, to promote his education, enhance his professional pride, enlarge good feeling with his professional brethren, and give him a proper sense of the duties belonging to the profession and the public. The medical man needs advancement in the general knowledge of the duties, the rights, and the privileges that surround him while occupying so imporant a position. The man of public and professional pretensions is measured by a rigid and exact rule, and if he fails to give good measure, he stands disgraced and his professional brethren around him. Every member should consider that the weight of good character, professional reputation, position, and influence in his profession, is beyond estimation.

The whole community looks to medical men for the solution of all dark and difficult problems of a scientific and medical nature. These questions are unliminated in their range, taking in the character of diseases and similations, questions of a sexual bearing, the sanitary condition of cities and towns, identity, legitimacy, death, real or apparent, homicide; poisons, the various kinds and how used; business transactions, civil and criminal: the highest interests of individuals, families, and society, frequently rest on medical men, not only of property and life, but that which is equally dearer, character and reputation. These things should induce us to search after knowledge and truth all our days, and when found apply it for the good of mankind. "Our work is great, self-sacrificing, and a benevolent one; but it is sublime, even God-like, dealing with disease, pain, life and death."

It is pleasant to know that the members of this Society

have been ever faithful in their duties; but still, events are before; the interests of humanity are here; the hopes of the profession of our State are in this Society; may we act well our part under such circumstances!

We should think of the centuries that have elapsed, since the records began, of the thoughts, the experience, and the researches of so many men, as to medicine and their uses, that are preserved for us. By organization we are encouraged to wrest something daily from science, literature and art to increase our stores of knowledge. Attachment to this course of life will soon determine the question as to our success and our influence in the world for good.

Knowledge has no limit, because the Great Author is without limit in knowledge and power. During all the past ages of the world, as man progressed, the various arts and sciences with which he was connected, yielded to the same omnipotent influence. In no age of the world's history have there been presented more evidence of the development of this law than at present. Indeed all animate nature, as well as man, the last and greatest of God's works, obeyed this law with precision and fidelity from age to age. Discoveries already made can in no way lessen the domain of new discoveries, "until time shall be no longer;" nay, the discovery of new knowledge is a productive parent of new acquisitions; and a new era of science, but the precursor of another, more lofty and beautiful, to be gained step by step.

With all our attainments in knowledge, as to forms and substances or material knowledge, there is still much to learn. Physiology has been re-created, and pathology born again. We may say the same of chemistry, therapeutics, anatomy, obstetrics, the science and practice of medicine and surgery. The whole wide circle lies open before us, and the acquisition of all these is important to the physician to enable him to do good to others, and adorn his professional character. This knowledge can only be secured by cumulative labors in the departments of generalization, induction, and experiments. Let us trace the history of any one department of science, and mark the primary germs of it; we must acknowledge that it is the fruit of a vineyard cultivated by many laborers; a superstructure of fixed principles of truth, added gradually by different minds. No one with whom we are acquainted could have attained his present perfection and magnitude by the efforts and labors of a single intelligence; therefore, the more laborers and the more thorough the devotion, the more perfect the knowledge and the more successful the practical application of the principles established by such means.

If we examine carefully the science and the art, the study and practice of medicine, as it is at the present day, we will see the importance of every one who assumes the responsibility of dealing with the lives and the happiness of his fellow-creatures, of seeking that association where he will receive light to guide him in searching after knowledge and truth.

It is with deep regret that we see our noble profession suffer by the partial and superficial education of many who enter the ranks. This can only be avoided by a careful inquiry into the preliminary studies and intellect of the student, by the private preceptors and medical *faculties*, before admission, as well as making the course of study more exact and more thorough. The student should possess transcendent merit, great devotion to study, and love for the profession, with profound judgment. These are the prerequisites to success, and few fail who possess these qualifications. This is the only way to elevate professional character, and meet the following requirements of the American Medical Association, that "every individual, on entering the profession, as he becomes thereby entitled to all its privileges and immunities, incurs an obligation to exert his best abilities to maintain its dignity and honor, and to exalt its standing."

Physicians should always feel that their profession requires a high toned, dignified and honorable course of conduct with their professional brethren, with their patients and with the world. They should be intelligent and courteous gentlemen, generous and warm-hearted friends, trustworthy and public spirited citizens, kind and accommodating neighbors, whole-souled philanthropists, earnest, sincere and steadfast Christians, ardent lovers of their country, thoroughly devoted to every moral and benevolent movement, always endeavoring to be an ornament in all things amongst the great and good, observing strictly the laws which are instituted for the government of the profession, and follow the golden rule, "Do to others as you would wish they should do to you." The importance of these high qualifications in the physician will be seen when we investigate his surroundings. "He must necessarily see and hear a great deal that none should ever see or know, save the family where the matter occurs." He sees much that glitters before the world, become the merest dross in the sick chamber. He sees, too, the gold shining bright in the crucible of affliction. He sees human passion in every form and condition; implacable hatred, and love as strong as death; fallen virtue, and virtue tried and proved; mental and moral strength, and childish imbecility in the once mighty and great; hope beaming bright with heavenly lustre, and ghastly fear, and black despair; unbounded power of endurance, and the broken spirit; with these scenes before him, and conscious of the responsibility and confidence reposed in him, he should maintain the honor of his profession and a dignified course in the community. In endeavoring to fulfil this duty, he must protect the interests of his medical compeers; for a physician, writhing under the pinching pangs of poverty, cannot successfully prosecute scientific or literary investigations; nor can he, with pleasure to himself, nor with success to his patients, prosecute the practice of his profession. Self-preservation is the first and paramount law of nature, and I know of nothing that is more preservative in its character than the means by which our physical wants are to be supplied. To provide for one's self and his household is a divine law: and he is pronounced worse than an infidel who does not do it.

Our wants and those of our families must, in some degree, be met, before the rugged cliffs of science can be surmounted, or the open fields of literature surveyed.

A physician does nothing by proxy, and therefore derives no gains but from his own individual efforts; a faithful attention to business is not sufficient alone, but an arrangement should be made for the prompt collection of fees. A man feels some gratitude immediately after he recovers from disease, but he will soon forget the means that were used for his recovery. It is better to have no business than one which does not pay. Again, the expertness and excellence attained by practice and experience, should never be used to the injury of the timid and less experienced in practice or surgery.

It is often difficult to establish professional fame, but its worth is in proportion to its cost. To elevate an edifice of renown requires both time and labor; but in an effort to do it every false means and every course should be avoided which is calculated to detract from the reputation of a brother practitioner, and we should observe under all circumstances the most honorable course of medical ethics. This course gives all who are well qualified for their profession, the power to be useful and happy, with habits and manners of gentlemen—earnest in the work of extending the bounds of medical science, picking up the ablest and best material, to advance their own interests, and to know how fearfully and wonderfully man is made, which is the command of religion and of science as well as the dictates of reason.

The application of the mind with diligence is necessary, not only for acquiring knowledge, but for securing the honors and emoluments which are its rewards.

As we cast our eyes back over the important events of the past ages of the world, we see the gradual, but steady, development of the healing art. The master stream having been formed by the coalescing and union of the best minds in every age, gathering the results of experiments and researches along the declivities of time down to the present day. But all the discoveries and improvements of preceding generations have been surpassed by the achievements of the present age.

And with all the attainments made in medical knowledge, there is still much to learn. All things earthly have a great influence on man's physical as well as his intellectual and moral usefulness. We should hasten then to gather into the treasury of our minds every solid ore and every precious gem that will increase our power to do good; this will protect us against idleness, routinism, and self-conceit, and encourage us to know medicine from foundation to coping-stone. Let us look at these consequences of routinism and self-conceit. "The routinist practices without any philosophical principle or foundation to guide him, reasoning solely on the perception of his senses; he is aged in his ideas, regardless of the progress of science, and obstinately confines himself within a limited circle of certain actions. All his knowledge and ability consist in laying hold of the first appearance of things, and in prescribing certain formulæ. He also becomes indolent and indisposed to everything that requires labor; his intellect is never applied to reflection, and as to observation and deduction from every-day occurrences in his practice, he is a perfect stranger. He declaims against all investigation and improvement in medical science, and is too stupid and proud to recognize anything valuable in the profession around him. Blind to every principle of pathology and therapeutics, he approaches the bedside of his patient, with ignorance and death standing by his side whispering, *all chance*. These physicians pretend to diagnose disease at a single glance; they hasten to the bedside of their patient, and ask a few questions for form's sake, and make the same prescription perhaps a score of times in a day, no difference what disease they meet with."

Again, we see the self-conceited, equally contemptible and degrading to the profession. He has a blind headstrong confidence in his own qualifications; he scoffs at medical associations of every kind, discards the idea of improvement there. "He is wiser than his teachers," and every other person he has knowledge of. He pretends to have read everything, has seen everything, is the most scientific and successful practitioner in the land; "The most difficult surgical operations are to him mere pastime;" constantly speaking of himself and his mighty achievements; nothing to him is obscure—all the secrets of nature are to him easily discovered; for no veil hides from his far-seeing eye the mysteries of our organization; new discoveries to him are worthless, for already he knows everything that does or can afflict the human frame.

If he is met in consultation, he has impudence enough to disregard the laws of etiquette, pretend to detect at once the most delicate lesions, and vauntingly puff the unequalled prescriptions secreted from his own brain. Such is the material that opposes medical organizations. These degrading presumptions can only be effectively avoided by mutual and daily intercourse and investigation with high-minded and scientific men of our calling; men of transcendant merit, always respecting the laws of the profession. The natural roughness of our nature will be polished by this kind of social intercourse; this, rightly understood and practiced, makes physicians taste the pleasures of their profession truly.

See that isolated physician who knows no place but his office, and no companions but his books. He goes into the sick room awkward and ignorant; his demeanor manifests his qualities at once; his patients lose confidence in him; he always appears to disadvantage, and is not likely to be a successful practitioner. He may have good talents and profound knowledge, but is not likely to occupy a high position in the profession. If he possesses the qualities that make a gentleman, and pursues this course of life, he is sure to become timid and unhappy in the practice of his profession; the most simple cases will alarm him; he will always act in fear, never satisfied with his prescriptions, constantly changing them; he will rarely attack disease at the right time, or with the proper remedies. His timidity causes him to withhold his treatment until the period of recovery is frequently passed. Such men do not kill their patients, but they let them die. If they would join their brethren in medical organization and labor with them diligently in the good work, they would undoubtedly get rid of much of their timidity. This course with attention to the study and practice of their profession would give the communities, where they reside, an opportunity to appreciate their worth. No physician should be content with the general intelligence of the masses, but should endeavor to bring forth additional information regarding the laws of hygiene and the curative processes, embracing, within the expansive folds of science, every known thing that is useful; and to establish at every point a fresh, able and determined advocate and defender of the noble profession of medicine—a profession, so often traduced, has done more to render life long and happy than any other.

To sustain such a profession in obedience to the great law of progress, and to contribute to its usefulness in the right direction, should be our constant aim and effort.

Our science alone discloses the truth of those mysterious processes and forces, as well as the physical and intellectual constitution of man, both as a creature perfect in structure and attributes, and as a moral and physical ruin. Therefore the practical result of our skill is to inform the human family as to the best mode of preserving their health in natural perfection, and giving counsel as to the physical training and education of the youth, according to the necessities of society; controlling disease in all its dangerous forms, that threaten the domestic altar. This is a great estate, the riches grasped out of fleeting centuries, and the most valuable of possessions.

With the riches and power of this estate, it gives administrative and executive power over the whole human family; and what gives additional honor to the physician, is, that he is the protector and friend of the poor and the distressed in every rank;

and by precept and example raising them up to the level of his own excellency, wealth and power which it creates and maintains. Take from the physician the motive that should actuate his course, a desire to benefit his fellow creatures, and you crumble to atoms the foundation of his profession. It is that elevating principle that induces him to risk his own life, if necessary, to save that of his patient. It has been done on the field of battle to save the wounded—it has been done where the most virulent, contagious and malignant diseases were sweeping entire districts—it has been done in the prosecution of the studies essential to the performance of the duties of an enlightened physician. Many never think, that in their calling, they exhibit virtues that in other positions would crown them with laurels and draw the admiration of the world. Others, conscious of their good traits, shun admiration, and quietly seek the good of their fellow-beings.

The value of the skill and motives of a physician will be more intelligible, when we consider the generally received principle of law as connected with the liberty and usefulness of the members of every community—"that each person naturally has a legal right to the enjoyment of his life, limbs, property and reputation." As this right is natural and inherent, it cannot be destroyed or disabled without a manifest breach of civil liberty. For the preservation of these rights, the law requires the thorough education of those whose talents and time are to be devoted to this end—securing them a just remuneration in return. If a person professes to possess certain qualifications and expresses a readiness to perform them, he is justly liable to the law if he fails to perform them; and that he shall exhibit continuous study and an accurate knowledge of the improvements of the day, with a proper regard for the responsible position, embracing all that is essential in preserving the health and protecting the lives of the community where he labors. Here we see combined obligations—destroy these, and we would have something like the savage tortures practiced in the dark ages, rendering the practitioner unfit to associate with refined and polished society. The profession must fully comprehend its duties and responsibilities, and proper and special qualifications for the practice of medicine, before any attempt can succeed to get the public to appreciate what these are, or to acknowledge the impropriety of using secret remedies. If we make no distinction between the regular and irregular practitioner, between the physician and the proprietor of a nostrum, we are censurable that two such characters are confounded by the community. Until the profession is united, and honestly cultivate a proper spirit in our calling, it is vain to expect a change of public opinion regarding medical science.

To prevent disease, and treat those that are diseased, is a benevolent and honorable vocation, and to conceal for selfish purposes a valuable remedy, displays a dishonest principle, void of philanthropy, placing a moneyed valuation upon pain and life. Such an individual may profess what he pleases, but a fact is established, that with him the almighty dollar is above the physical sufferings of his fellow beings; his piety is not divine—for that teaches us to eschew evil, and love our neighbor as ourselves. Another cause of the unjust reproach and odium that the ignorant and degraded in almost every community cast against the medical profession, is from want of interest and zeal in members of medical organizations. Let all who are indifferent, or opposed in any way to the united action of the profession, examine their position, and they will find that they are encouraging quackery of every color. This Society asks nothing but what is strictly just, and what every regular member owes to it. To stand separate from medical organizations is opposing the better elements of the means that dignify and adorn our calling; it is giving encouragement to quacks and all kinds of quackery; it is standing on the side of ignorance and against improvement, a mere mercenary machine, ready to grovel in the pit of infamy, for selfish purposes. Opposition to this best means of increasing our knowledge and usefulness is on an equality with the so-called D. D.'s, M. D.'s and LL. D.'s, who lend themselves and their influence to promote the sale of various nostrums—attesting falsehoods of the baser sort for the benefit of impostors and humbugs. These, in connection with that portion of the press which has no higher object than filthy lucre, feed the weak minded with the most miserable trash, in the form of demoralizing books and advertisements in the public journals, appending high-sounding titles and false statements to the articles offered. This infamous practice is carried to such an extent at the present day, as to poison both mind and conscience, destroying the morality of both sexes of the rising generation. Such persons giving their influence in connection with and through the press, become willing criminals for the sacrifice of human life. And I may mention one more of like character, and cheerfully would I pass by this disgraceful field and save the feelings of this intelligent audience around me, but the bold and unprincipled efforts to give notoriety to this imposition during the last few years, requires a passing notice.

The efforts to impose on our brave and patriotic soldiers with the *"like cure like"* system is still fresh in our memories. Think of a brave soldier defending the cause of his country, carried off the field of battle wounded with a deadly missile; another is bleeding to death from a severed artery; the "like cure like" surgeon comes along—would he, or dare he apply, or resort to the treatment they proclaim to the world? If he resorts to proper measures under such circumstances, and closes the gaping wound and ligates the wounded artery, he thereby declares to the world that their principles of treatment are false, that the system they represent is the basest humbug the world has ever seen, a disgrace to manhood, repugnant to common sense, opposed to every principle of science, and contrary to all reliable experience in the physical, mental and moral world. It is shocking to the better feelings of our nature, when we hear professors of religion—and doubly so, when we hear teachers in the Christian Church—speak favorably or advocate the "like cure like" system. This accounts for the want of confidence placed in many divines, because they disgrace their sacred calling by neglecting the doctrines of the bible and lend their aid and influence to impostors. When the Physician of souls visited the earth, He treated the body also. We are bound to believe that His whole course of life was strictly consistent. Who dare say when He met the blasphemer, the Sabbath breaker, the covetous, the drunkard, the extortioner, or any and all the corrupt wretches met with in His journeyings, that he ever gave the least evidence of the "like cure like" system? To argue such doctrine is in opposition to every principle of truth, light, and knowledge. The pure Homœopathist may safely stretch himself erect and defy the cold-hearted atheist to go far beyond him in slandering the King of Glory.

For the self-same principle must and will come out the same. If the principle is right in regard to the body, it will apply to the immortal part of man. Such doctrine is wanton blasphemy, and cannot be tolerated by persons possessed of common-sense views of things sacred and divine.

We still remember the disgrace our nation suffered by the calling of such creatures to see a member of the Cabinet, in the capital of our country. But, by the mysterious workings of Divine Providence, the assassin's work opened the way to save his life, and save the nation from part of the disgrace.

The profession, as we represent it, has lived and flourished from the early ages. Charlatanism and quackery have endeavored to destroy true medicine with as much zeal as infidelity labored to destroy Christianity. But these cancroid and corroding enemies have been sloughed off in their fetid shape, and true medical science remains unmoved. None but an honest and pure profession could have resisted the impediments that ours has done, and lived. Then may we not be justly proud when we feel that our best efforts are used to sustain such a profession and contribute to its usefulness? Some may be discouraged when they consider the magnitude of the work, and look at their surroundings. None should despair, for a real love of learning and true ambition to be excellent in the profession will surely succeed. True greatness will always be acknowledged sooner or later. Sometimes it is late, because an opportunity is wanting for its conspicuous development; but during a lifetime that opportunity will occur.

To the physician, as to all others, if he is qualified for his duties, truly representing his noble profession—if he possesses the real element of solid knowledge and worth—there is a time when these qualifications will be proclaimed and acknowledged.

Physicians should begin their task understandingly, with a firm resolve to do their part in relieving the distressed, and maintaining the dignity and usefulness of the profession. Then nothing can hinder them from giving to the possession of learning, the practice of virtue, the attainment of public esteem and confidence. This is a sure foundation for happiness, built on an immovable rock. Without this all their enterprises are vain, and they shall be pointed at as persons of no judgment, no industry, no talents, no use in society, fit only to be cast aside, neglected, and despised by mankind. It may be truthfully said that a great physician is among the first of great men. He makes himself great by the improvements with which he perfects the healing art, and thus becomes the benefactor of humanity; by the power which he exercises over disease, and by the zeal which he manifests in his attempts to remove it. Every physician should appreciate these obligations in the practice of his profession.

If our calling is full of bitterness, the sweet pleasures of it, and its aims and hopes, banish and transcend the pain. The elevation and union of the profession are the best means of obtaining our desired object, and its growth will be increasing evidence of a check on imposition. Labor unseals the blind natural eye of man, and fills it with the light of knowledge. This, with the indomitable will, the prolonged search, the untiring patience, invigorates and strengthens persistency in the cause of knowledge and usefulness. The inattentive man may overlook it, the careless man undervalue it, or the indolent man neglect it. But in our profession the man of ability, prudence, and diligence will surely succeed. Sick people are so desirous of life and health, that the ignorant physician will stand the least chance of being thought of. This important truth should ever be kept in mind, that "merit is sure of its reward in this world."

This should induce "every member of the profession who would defend its claims to honor and usefulness, and win for himself a distinguished position in its ranks, to assist, by every legitimate means, the organization of our noble profession for the advancement of medical knowledge," and assist each other to bear the sacrifice and endure the labor which its successful prosecution demands. This is no trifling work; it is not a short work, nor an easy work. We should make no calculation to reach our aim short of a lifetime spent in earnest, honest, and self-sacrificing work. For the enemies of light and truth are always busy, and will always be busy. They are united, and will be united. The innumerable hosts of *pathies* and *isms* are all combined against true medicine and are endeavoring to add to their number, and will add to their number daily, while the practitioner of true medicine looks on with indifference. We may well say to those without organization: Why stand by idle? There is a day coming when you must give an account of your stewardship, and what did you do with your talents? Our work is dignified, it is noble, it is honorable. That man must be a fool who refuses to enlist in a cause that benefits the human race, and there is no fool on earth equal to the professional fool: he dwarfs his manhood and insults common sense.

Every physician should consider the good he is capable of doing, by proper application and by continued endeavors to relieve suffering and sorrowing humanity, and bearing an honorable part in the constant conflict between truth and error.

between right and wrong. What cause is better than an honest desire to restore fallen manhood, alleviate suffering, and correct the evils that distress and destroy the human race?

The soul of man is, in this world, like the dove on the wide waters of the flood, without a resting place. There is no point of repose, and the surest way to escape sorrow and trouble is to labor assiduously in the path of knowledge with an earnestness for future good.

Man, goverened and influenced by this principle, will surely obey the eternal law, to become dignified, and elevate himself in the scale of creation, physically, mentally and morally, to the end of his days, feeling that when released from the affairs and circumstances of time, he is still destined to a spiritual elevation throughout all eternity.

SCLEROSIS OF THE NERVE CENTRES.

Sclerosis of the Nerve Centres is a condition of the structure and cause of various forms of diseases that has been taxing the best efforts of the Pathological Anatomist and Physiologist in all parts of the medical world for several years. Although much has been discovered, and many former mysteries connected with the symptoms and cause of many nervous affections have been accounted for and explained, yet the morbid conditions which relate specially to this subject and positive knowledge of all changes and phenomena brought about by induration of the nerve centres are comparatively incomplete.

The term, Sclerosis, in a limited sense meaning hard, and nerve centres, a restricted field, will necessarily bring me within the range of diseases affecting the nervous system connected with the brain and spinal cord. As all the normal phenomena of the living organism are known to occur under the influence of the nervous system, and are controlled by it, so it is but reasonable to regard all morbid actions as being more or less influenced by diseased nervous action. We might here state that the actions of the cerebro-spinal system are subject to cessation and interruption, while those of the ganglionic system are of a continuous and uninterrupted character. Let us look briefly at the two grand divisions of the nervou system; the cerebro-spinal system embracing all the aesthetics, intellectual and senso-motory phenomena, and the ganglionic, governing the circulatory, secretory and nutritive acts in their widest sense; the sensory element of the cerebro-spinal system by an intimate and active reflex relation; under certain influences and circumstances; controls the ganglionic even to the complete subversion of its healthful reign in the animal economy.

This nervous system, thus constituted with all its delicate and well appointed arrangements; its inherent powers, and its reflex susceptibilities is subjected constantly to aggressions from the external world; its thermal, luminous, electric hygrometric, and toxic conditions; all more or less coming in relation with it, to depress, or to exalt, to paralyze or disturb both its direct and indirect energies. But beside being subjected to the external world, it is subjected to an internal world, whose influences are equally powerful—that vast and all pervading domain, the blood. Now it is my desire to point out the characteristics of the disease under consideration and the peculiar effects on the healthy economy, as far as we find it located in the nerve centres.

Sclerosis corresponds to affections in other parts called by different names, but always meaning hard or indurated. It is characterized by the hyperaplasia of the interstitial nerve cement or connective tissue. The increased density of the structure, sometimes the consistence does not exceed concrete albumen, in others the consistence of cheese, and in a few of a cartilaginous character, these forms are generally found in spots. The proximate cause is undoubtably a deposition of lymph into the connecting tissue by which the inter-moleculor intervals are filled up and cemented together, supposed to result from chronic inflammation.

When it effects the brain, as a general rule it is found in the white or medullary substance of the brain; not often in the cortical substance, with greyish white nodules and a fibrillated appearance showing fragments of new fibres—granular masses—nucleated cells, such as are seen in atrophied nerve structure; most generally the disease is found in scattered patches through the brain in nodules from the size of a pea to that of an almond. Sometimes sclerosis and softening of the brain are associated together, and patches of grey induration and grey degeneration blended with inflammatory products, as to make the mass like a new growth. Occasionally a case is found where the disease extends over an entire lobe or an entire hemisphere. The disease may be limited to the brain, but often the brain and spinal cord at the same time.

Then there is an occasional sclerosis of the whole brain as described by Bright in his Medical Report. In a little girl that lay perfectly motionless and senseless for a year before her death with her limbs stiffly extended and without the possibility of her making the slightest movement the white substance of the brain was found after death as hard as soft cartilage, so that the grey substance could be peeled off it, leaving the mould of the convolutions in the white substance. A stream of water washed off the grey matter leaving the convolutions below on the hard white substance, giving it the appearance of a wax model of a brain. The ventricles looked as if they had been modeled in wax. The white passed in streaks into the grey convolutions around. The cord was also hardened.

Symptoms of the brain trouble are generally manifested in the mutual condition; the faculties of the brain are more or less enfeebled, the memory generally fails, headache, vertigo and melancholy are prominent features, and like other lesions of the substances of the brain, give rise to paralysis. When paralysis takes place from this cause the muscles are effected gradually by the dissemination of the lesion which causes the paralysis, and by the successive occurance of sclerosed nodules. Generally at first the paralysis is confined to certain of the muscles of one of the lower limbs, then certain musles of an upper limb, or of a corresponding muscle of the opposite side. Paralysis may extend to the trunk. Strabismus may occur. The muscles involved in speech, in deglutition and respiration may become implicated. The cutaneous sensibility may be but little affected. Defective vision and deafness are occasional effects.

Muscular tremor is a very contstant symptom. It precedes and accompanies paralytic effects. During the progress of the disease, convulsive movements are observed and co-ordinating powers frequently become defective. Nutrition of the body may continue and even grow fat. In this connection I will refer to a case reported in the Epileptic Hospital, New York. The patient had been an Epileptic from youth, and for months before his death had a feeling of dizziness in his head. The brain tissue was in a general state of sclerosis; under the microscope the nervous elements appeared deficient, and replaced by connective cells and fibres. More particularly in the medulla oblongata. The anterior and lateral columns were partially degenerated.

Now we may consider the same kind of lesions taking place within the spinal cord. Corresponding to those we were considering as taking place within the cranium. Sclerosis of the spinal cord is supposed to proceed from chronic inflammation— a specific diathesis or peculiar constitutional defect, and consists in an abnormal production of the connective tissue of the nerve substance involving more or less atrophy and other degenerative changes in the nervous structure; these altertaions are of a notable hardness and of a greyish color. The sclerosis may be limited to a single segment of the cord. Existing in isolated patches more or less numerous and deficeincy in size in different cases—distinguished as irregular, diffused or multiple sclerosis. Again we find sclerosis in the anterior portion of the cord, sometimes in the lateral portions of the cord, and the sclerosis may be seated exclusively in the posterior columns. Each column affected extending over a greater or less space. When limited in extent, the lumber section is most generally affected. Again the lesion may exist in the anterior and lateral portions at the same time. Although the tendency of sclerosis of the cord is to progress in a given anatomical tract, yet the disease may be of a coarser kind and attack several parts of the cord at the same time; and sclerosis of the spinal cord and brain are not infrequently associated.

Sclerosis of the antero-lateral portions of the cord give rise to general paralysis and paraplegia; these portions contain the fibres which transmit volitions to the muscles of the extremities. It would seem that the disease in this part of the cord interferes with the motor function in such a way that the forces are transmitted in an irregular manner to the muscle. This form of disease has long been confounded with paralysis agitans; but is now known to be a distinct affection, both in its pathology and symptoms. It is now believed that paralysis agitans depends on a want of innervation, and sclerosis in a change of tissue with rhythmical movements, and has a more rapid course and terminates by spasm and contraction of the limbs. The disease differs from paralysis agitans in being observed most frequently in young people, it commences by feebleness in walking as in some forms of paraplegia, but there is no loss of power over the rectum and bladder; nor is there any loss of sensibility as generally met with in ataxia. After some months the tottering gait and feebleness increase until the energies of the patient are altogether impaired and the disease is fully developed. When this has occured, we are struck with the remarkable regular or rhythmical movements of the body and limbs. At night jerking and darting pains running up and down the legs; sometimes a feeling of compression about the abdomen as if a cord were drawn around it. This disease in the motor tracts often extends upwards into the cranium and even reaches the brain proper; then the muscles of the face become affected and the ordinary expression is lost. This will be readily seen in the action of the arms. If the arm is attempted to be held out, it moves slowly and in an orderly manner, so that if the patient be told for example to put a spoon to his mouth, the arm will ascend in regular stages, until the mouth is reached, when if the spoon is put in, it will clatter against the teeth. The movements are best observed during the action of the muscles of speech; the words are brought out one by one, or syllable by syllable as a child learning to read. This interrupted or jerking mode of talking is characteristic of this affection. If the patient be sitting up, his head also may be seen moving in a regular manner. The eyes are also constantly rolling from side to side. If the head is supported and the body is at rest there is no movement; but in a case of paralysis agitans the movements cease only during sleep.

In the sclerosis of which I am speaking, it is only when the patient rises from bed that his head and shoulders undergo an oscillatory motion. There is a difference in the intellect: In sclerosis it is simply impaired without any of the positive delusions which exist in general paralysis; the patient is not always depressed; frequently happy; generally emotional and ready to laugh or cry when spoken to. After the continuance of these symptoms for sometime, the next stage commences, the legs become stiff and the patient is unable to walk; he takes to his bed, the legs are stretched out and absolutely rigid; sometimes the legs are bent up and stiff, but more generally they are stretched out straight: there is no weakness of the bladder or rectum, as in paraplegia, nor do bed sores appear; there is no loss of sensation; this form of the disease generally lasts from two to three years.

Dr. S. Weir Mitchell describes anterior or lateral sclerosis as having little or no tremor when at rest; the few vibrations are rapid and short; but are intensified when the patient attempts to carry a cup to the lips in the act of drinking, or any other volitional act. In summing up these symptoms it may be as well to state in this connexion what the scalpel and microscope has revealed after these symptoms were witnessed. There was found after death a chronic myelitis or hyperplasia of the nerve substance—sclerosed masses of connective tissue scattered through the anterior or motor columns of the cord, often reaching as high as the corpora striata, and passing into the brain itself; these were mostly of a pinkish grey color, not well defined from the surrounding tissue, into which they gradually pass. A section of the cord will display these grey patches of various shapes and sizes; and in sections of the cerebral hemispheres they become well marked in contrast with the white medullary matters.

We may now look at sclerosis of the posterior columns of the cord. According to our present knowledge, the posterior column is intimately related to the cerebellum, and by means of short fibres connect one portion of the grey centres with another; it also propagates the influence of that part of the encephalon, which combines with the nerves of volition to regulate the locomotive powers and serve to harmonize the actions of the several segments of the cord; and as pathological changes correspond very often to distinct anatomical regions, and as these changes are accompanied by special characteristic symptoms in chronic myelitis, grey degeneration or sclerosis of the posterior columns of the spinal cord, we have a want of co-ordination, and by the loss of this regulating power of the body we witness the complaint known as locomotor ataxy. Sir William Gull describes patients laboring with this disease that they could not walk in a straight line; they threw their limbs forward and had great difficulty in turning round; there was often a numbness of common sensation, so that the patient could not direct the muscles, and considered it an actual weakness in their contraction.

Dr. Chenne designated the disease as a progressive abolition of co-ordination of the movement and integrity of the muscular force. The same facts apply to the arms; the patient cannot make a straight-forward thrust, for the arms will strike from side to side; they are deep seated aching pains; to use the common expression of patients, they were seated in the bones; sometimes instead of being constant or enduring like those of rheumatism they resemble electric shocks, darting through the limbs or muscles.

Charcot considers the degeneration or sclerotic change mostly limited to the outer portions of the posterior columns, avoiding the tracts next to the lateral fissure. In a few cases the posterior roots of the nerves have been found involved in the disease. The membranes, too, may be thickened and adherent.

Vulpian speaks of four autopsies. That in all these cases the sensitive nerves were found completely normal, also the posterior roots between the ganglia and point of junction with the anterior; but between the ganglion and the spinal cord, these same roots were atrophied invariably, when the posterior columns of the cord were sclerosed. It would seem that the ganglion interposed a barrier to the progress of the disease along the spinal roots. Had the disease affected the anterior roots, destitute of a ganglion we might suppose that it would have extended to the periphery. Now I have described to you the effects of this disease in its pure and simple form. It is not to be understood as designating ataxy to every form of spinal affection, for you may easily suppose that if this disease is due to the changes described, such morbid changes may affect other portions of the cord and produce a complex case; but the most recent investigation in pathological anatomy has shown that a large proportion of the cases of locomotor ataxy results from grey degeneration or sclerosis of the posterion columns of the spinal cord.

No doubt many might think these views more positive than our present knowledge of sclerosis will justify, for it has been well established that paralysis, anaesthesia, amaurosis, aphasia, chorea and epilepsy have resulted from hemorrhage by the rupture of arterial branches in the nerve structure by new formations, tumors, malignant and benign; softening of the brain or spinal cord, or both, as well as by sclerosis; but in a large proportion of such cases they are accompanying symptoms and circumstances that will throw light on the cause of change in the nerve centres. And now to consider the indirect effect of this disease viz: The changes that may take place in the organs controlled mostly by the ganglionic system. The ophthalmic ganglion is connected with branches of the third and fifth pairs of nerves; the spheno-palatine ganglion with branches of the fifth and seventh pairs of nerves; the sub-maxillary ganglion with the fifth and seventh pairs of nerves; the otic ganglion with the fifth and seventh pair; the cervical ganglions with the cervical spinal nerves, and all the ganglia in the chest and abdomen are connected with the cerebro-spinal nerves, and as this great sympathetic system is distributed to organs over which the consciousness and the will have no immediate control.

The liver, spleen, kidneys, supra renal, capsules, large and small intestines, obtain their nervous supply mostly from the ganglionic system, but the roots of their sympathetic branches uniting with the cerebro-spinal centres by numerous attachments so that mechanical or altered nerve structures in the cerebro-spinal nerve centres, will influence these various organs in the same manner as in local irritation, give rise to altered circulation, nutrition and secretion; to chemical change in the fluids and tissues, and of temperature, and the constitution of the blood. Amongst the most important causes may be considered the partial loss of the vital force and thereby a general impairment of the functions of the different organs. Take, for example, the effects that result from division of the pneumogastric nerves; this experiment is invariably followed by a suspension of the arterializing process; the same effect has been observed by merely tying these nerves. If you open the carotid artery after ligating the phrenic nerves, the blood that flows has a dark color; take away the nervous influence from the blood and it will become darker and darker, until at length the lungs are rendered utterly incompetent to make any salutary impression upon it. The inflammations and ulcerations in the kidney, and the mucous membrane of the bladder after injuries of the medulla spinalis; the extensive abdominal inflammations after sections of the thalamus opticus; peritonitis and nephritis connected with inflammation of the spinal cord; gastro enteritis in inflammation or softening of the brain, and softening of the stomach in meningitis of the base of the brain. These all go to show the intimate, and to a great extent dependent relation the various organs hold to the cerebro-spinal system.

And now a few words about this communicating link. Our modern physiologists tell us that the different forms of disturbance referred to are due to irritation, and not cessation in the function of the various parts of the brain; for irritation of parts around the portion impaired or destroyed by disease causes certain sensations, not that the part destroyed causes them, but because an irritation starting from the place around influences cells, some near, some at a considerable distance from the locality of the lesion; believing therefore that certain functions of the brain instead of being localized in clusters of cells are on the contrary spread over the greater part, if not the entire brain. This theory explains a very large number of the cases of disease referred to, which would otherwise be very difficult to understand. Parts in the brain supposed to be endowed with special functions can be destroyed without any loss of function; so that it follows that any part of the brain can produce loss of power and parts supposed to contain special functions can be destroyed without loss of power.

It makes no difference whatever, whether the distance be small or much greater, as in either case their communications with each other must take place by nerve fibres, the length of which is unable to interfere with the function. Each half of the brain is a complete brain originally, and possesses an aptitude to be developed as a centre for the two sides of body in volitional movements, as well as in all other cerebral functions.

Communication between the body and the brain can be more or less fully accomplished by means of a very much smaller number of conductors than are generally supposed. We know that the will gives an order and as we know by clinical facts that any part of the medulla oblongata can be destroyed without paralysis, and that in some cases a very small portion of it has proved sufficient for the persistence of voluntary movements; it would seem that the order may be transmitted as well by one fibre as by another, and that it is necessary to recognize the existence of faculties of a much higher order in the nerve cells of the spinal cord, than those that are admitted to exist there. Many facts and similar reasoning tend also to show that the nerve cells of the spinal cord possess as regards sensibility; faculties of a higher order than those which physiologists admitted a few years ago.

PYEMIA.

Pyemia is generally understood as a mixture of pus in the blood—giving rise to septicemia or blood poison. Pus is the direct cause of the affection we are now considering, and it is altogether proper, that we should examine some of the causes of this product.

It is a well settled belief at the present day that pus is the result of the inflammatory action; either acute or chronic, simple or specific. The causes are very numerous and no period of life is exempt from it. The infant at the breast and the advanced in years have suffered with inflammatory disturbance followed by suppuration. Pus is composed of serum fibrin and the globules of the blood changed by inflammation—the fluid part of pus has properties not found in serum. The gastric juice of animals will not coagulate pus. Muriate of ammonia will coagulate the fluid part of pus; but not other secretions or natural fluid. There is some difference in the products from serous and mucous surfaces, and also from the various morbid conditions which surround the tissue. It is also modified by the presence of extraneous substances—grumous blood fibrin, cholestein, or the debris of organs and textures. It is heavier than water; about as heavy as blood; it is susceptible of absorption, and is frequently removed by the absorbent vessels, supposed to undergo a species of disintegration, and is carried off by the liver, kidneys and other channels. Prior to the formation of pus, we have effusion of serum, effusion of lymhp, adhesion, hardening, with undue heat, swelling, pain, perverted secretion and sensibility, and finally suppuration; and these with the constitutional and local causes are further modified by many specific impressions, giving rise to the primary inflammation. During these changes, sometimes the parts around become organized into a sac, lined by a membrane called pyogenic membrane; this membrane may secrete more pus, or absorb some of it. Pus diffused through the natural textures, tends to soften and separate them and break them down. For convenience I will divide pus into healthy and unhealthy. Healthy pus contains albumen, extractive matter, fatty matter, salts of lime and soda; the globules are a little larger than the red corpuscles of blood; there are several kinds of unhealthy pus: the ichorous, sanious, curdy, slimy, serous malignant and contagious pus. Connected with the diffusion and absorption of some form of unhealthy pus lies the great danger to health and life. When disease attacks either the suppurating surface or the constitution, the character of the pus generally changes, often becoming putrid. Poisonous principles may be incorporated in the pus without detection, for chemistry has failed to detect or show any difference between pus of gonorrhœa, syphilis, malignant pustule, glanders and small pox, and pus from a common abscess. I will not discuss the theories under investigation at the present day such as bacteria, micrococci, microgerms, the microsporina supposed to produce diphtheria, or the monadina that brings on inflammation, but for convenience will consider pyemia connected with the practice of medicine, and next in surgery, and lastly in the parturient patients.

Pus frequently follows inflammation of the brain and membranes, and clinical experience has shown that abscess of the liver often follows with a large mortality. Pyemia follows many cases of pneumonia, pleurisy, typhoid fever, scarlet fever, dysentery, erysipelas, phlebitis, angriolucitis, small pox and carbuncle. In pneumonia the capillary vessels in the lungs give way sufficient to take up pus. In pleurisy the serous exudation is capable of resorption, but pus is not. In typhoid fever and dysentery the open ulcers in the alimentary canal take up pus rapidly. In erysipelas, phlebitis, angeiolucitis, scarlet fever and small pox the capillary vessels are largely destroyed, leaving open mouths for the reception of pus or other putrid substances. When inflammation takes place in the coats of the veins and capillary vessels, a watery, ichorous or sanious fluid mixes with the blood. the lining coat of the vessel is soon poisoned, and purulent collections soon follow and extend to the cellular tissue around, and in this way multiple abscesses form through the system, most common in the internal viscera. Prognosis very unfavorable.

Symptoms generally are chills, headache, low fever, frequent pulse, languor, thirst, confusion of thought, prostration, swelling of the joints, night sweats, edema of the lower extremities; the chilliness often amounts to shivering; heat in the palms of the hands and soles of the feet; pain in different parts of the body; skin sallow, sometimes jaundiced; indifference; in the advanced stage with cold extremities. A well marked change in the manner and appearance of the patient; the soreness often mistaken for rheumatism; if serous structure is affected the pain is generally severe; erysipelatous patches frequently appear on the surface. In the advanced stages of the diseases referred to, if the patient has chills irregularly, followed by profuse sweats, rapid and feeble pulse, low, persistent fever, sallowness of the skin, prostration, shifting pains, swelling of the joints and glands, cold abscessess and suppuration, the practitioner may conclude that pus is forming very rapidly in the deep seated viscera.

Treatment.—Much will depend on the primary cause and the general condition of the patient—but cleanliness, pure air and good nourishment will be proper in all cases. It is important to keep up the vital forces by nutriment and stimulants. Beef tea, good fresh milk, sometimes lime-water added, cream, eggs, oysters, wine, or what I consider better, pure rye whiskey, will be required in all bad cases, along with such medicinal agents to meet the condition of each patient according to the different changes that the patient may undergo. In cases following typhoid fever, sulphate of quinia and spirits of turpentine will be needed, and perhaps acetate of lead, opium and ipecac. will be necessary to control the complications; sulphite of soda with quinia will agree in a few cases; muriate and carbonate of ammonia will be useful when general alteratives are required; nitrate of silver introduced by Prof. Mitchell many years ago, and recently revived by Pepper, where ulcers were suspected in the bowels in the latest stages of typhoid fever and dysentery, has not been satisfactory in my hands.

The same remedies will be useful in cases following dysentery; after erysipelas muriate tincture of iron, chlorate of potash, muriate of ammonia and iodide of potassium are good remedies. Following scarlet fever, chlorine in some form is necessary; if the case becomes chronic, bichloride of mercury, muriate tincture of iron and Fowler's solution in combination is a good tonic and alterative compound. The same remedies with blisters will effect as much in phlebitis and angeiolucitis as any other course of treatment. Particular attention should be paid to the liver, kidneys, bowels and skin throughout the entire course of treatment—such remedies should be used as will keep them as near a healthy condition as possible. As the secretions almost always become vitiated, the food is seldom well digested. Pepsin or lactopeptine should be administered immediately after eating; this is a very important part of the treatment and should not be neglected.

Surgery.—In surgical cases we find many of the general symptoms the same—but modified by complications arising from other causes. Pyemia may follow any severe shock, or anything that suddenly depresses the vital powers, profuse hemorrhage, severe injuries of the head, gun-shot wounds, compound-comminuted and impacted fractures, injuries of the joints, dislocations, trephining, amputations, lithotomy, lithotrity, perineal section, operations for aneurism, hemorrhoids, extirpation of tumours of every kind, particularly where veins are wounded, and all extensive lacerations and contusions. Prognosis unfavorable.

Treatment.—All irritating causes should be removed as far as possible, and the system be well supported with tonics and stimulants. If there is an open suppurating surface, free drainage should be established and fomentations applied; if drainage should fail, the pyogenic membrane should be treated either with a solution of chlorinate of soda, dilute acid nitrate of mercury, tincture of iodine, balsam of Peru, or carbolized dressing. In compound fractures and all extensive wounds communicating with bones, balsam of Peru is generally the most satisfactory; all abscesses in reach should be opened, and soothing treatment to all inflamed parts not matured. Quinia is of more benefit in cases where septicemia follows a severe shock than in any other form; ammonia, iron, wine, whiskey, milk and animal broths in full quantities; opiates to relieve pain and procure sleep. If nausea is troublesome use ice and aromatic spirits of ammonia. If the stomach rejects opiates, the hypodermic use of morphia will be proper, and all the secretions should be cautiously guarded; tendencies to internal organs should be counteracted by dry cupping and counter irritation.

If hemorrhage takes place, ligatures, compression torsion, ferric alum, gallic acid and the astringent preparations of iron should be used to suit each individual case.

In all cases where the surgeon is called immediately to see a patient injured by accident, or where capital or severe operations are performed, he can save his patient much suffering and pain, and the risk of the dangers of septicemia, by the use of small doses of quinia, and alteratives to support the system and to keep the different organs healthy from the first treatment of the case. There is no doubt but much can be done to prevent septicemia by early attention to the symptoms leading to that result. In many cases quinia, opium and good nourishment will protect the patient. When the head is injured there is a strong tendency to disease of the liver; it is important to try and prevent abscess in that organ. Some of our modern surgeons are in favor of rectal alimentation when the stomach fails to bear food—it is well to try it; but experienced surgeons look upon all cases where the stomach rebels as exceedingly doubtful for recovery. As in general practice, lactopeptine should not be forgotten.

Parturient patients are different in many particulars from the cases met with in practice and surgery. The practitioner generally has the advantage of treating his patients before septicemia commences, and in a large proportion of his cases the patient had good health prior to the disease that laid the foundation for the blood-poison, and the symptoms during the course of the primary trouble, and the effects produced by the remedies administered, will assist in the management of the sequella. The surgeon meets with many patients that were healthy up to the day of the accident or the operation, and by commencing at the beginning of the case to protect his patient against all serioussequences, if not able to succeed successfully, he can certainly do more for his patient than where the system is saturated with pus before the patient is visited. Let us begin with our patient at conception and we find an inflammatory tendency during the whole period of pregnancy, and during this course, changes take place in the cavity of the abdomen; the blood is changed by the formation of keisteine, the secretion of milk, the fluid circulating through the fœtus, and perhaps some of the excretions of the embryo entering the blood of the mother, produces a tendency in the fluids to become acrid and putrid. Then the mental excitement, exhaustion of the brain or spinal cord, or both at the same time. Pressure on the renal veins and internal iliac causing exosmosis into the cellular tissues of the pelvis; the retention of urea, which a process of ferment produces carbonate of ammonia in the blood. This pressure and disturbance of the pelvic textures certainly interferes with the functions of assimilation, secretion and absorption, making a pathological condition in some of the parts; then old lesions only partially restored ready to start up again and increase the trouble and danger, such as cellulitis, granular disease of the mucous membrane, chronic metritis, scurvy, scrofula, tuberculosis; old dispacements such as prolapsis, anteversion, retroversion, retroflexion, hypertrophy, neuralgia, rheumatism, induration or ulceration; these conditions assist with atmospheric and toxic influences to lay the foundation for pyemia in parturient patients, either in miscarriage, abortion or labor at full term. When multiple abscesses are formed the contents seldom have pure pus, but the consistence of dirty grey plastic lymph mixed with grumous blood and flakes of fibrin; the parts around engorged with blood and frequently softened, but in some cases, and even fatal cases, the only changes discoverable are in the blood. After delivery at full term, the fatigue of gestation, the efforts of labor, the altered condition of all the structure within the pelvis and abdomen, the womb relieved of its weight and tension, and a large placental surface communicating by many orifices with the uterine sinuses and filled with plugs of coagula, the gravid organ returning to a non-gravid condition, the lining membrane to undergo fatty degeneration, the muscular tissue is to be reduced to small size, and the surplus fluids which pregnancy called into existence with the vessels and nerves are to be reduced by a process of absorption and exosmose to a normal condition. In some cases we have retained coagula or portions of retained placenta in different stages of decomposition, together with the pressed tissues, contusions, lacerations, ruptures and abraded surfaces; it is not at all strange that very slight morbid influences will lay the foundation for such inflammatory action as will result in blood poison. The whole course of a parturient case is more rapid and deceptive. There is no power left in the system to resist the decomposition and diffusion of the poisonous principles through every organ in the body, until the vital powers become so low that in a short time the mortal part is changed and wasted away. How deceptive are some of the symptoms: the tongue will sometimes be clean and moist until near the close; the bowels are generally at first costive till the vital force is low, then a profuse diarrhœa sets in, and is often uncontrollable; respiration rapid and short, pulse frequent and small, chills generally twice a day followed by heat and profuse perspiration; sometimes husky cough, glassy eye, dusky skin, coma, suppressed lochia and milk, urine scanty and often suppressed are the most prominent symptoms in this dread disease that prepares the victim for the change so unexpected to them. The experienced practitioner seldom meets with any form of disease where life and death are so strangely blended—where death takes the glow and hue of life—and life the distressed and grissly form of death. Prognosis—unfavorable.

Treatment.—Rest, good nursing, eliminatives, tonics, stimulants and nourishment covers the course of treatment. A patient saturated with poison and almost always brought low, from slow progressive changes in the system, needs all the rest and all the care possible to protect and preserve the small amount of vitality left—then to get rid of the putrid fluid that has poisoned and threatens to destroy the patient, has been a subject that has worried many practitioners. All will agree that it is right and proper to make an effort to remove the cause, but the course to pursue is not always clear. Good nursing with knowledge sufficient to administer the remedies prescribed as often as the patient can bear, is of the first importance. There are no class of patients cared for, that need experienced and good nursing more; everything used ought to be administered at the right time and in the right way---even minutes are important, and neglect for a very short time or imprudence on the part of the nurse may sacrifice a life. The knowledge to administer the remedies—to give stimulants and nourishment in proper quantities is of as much value as the services of the physician. Quinia-sulphite of soda, chlorate of potash, iodide of potassium, muriate of ammonia, spirits of turpentine, carbolic acid, salicine, salicylic acid, salicyllate of soda, sulpho-carbolate of soda and of zinc, have had their advocates. I have no doubt that in the great variety of cases met with, they may be all used to advantage, but when I speak for myself, quinia and chlorate of potash has been more satisfactory in my own experience than the other agents mentioned. I have not used all, nor have I visited patients where all were tried but have had reports from them. Muriate of ammonia is a good remedy, but I think a little slow—too slow I judge in the majority of cases. Spirits of turpentine is useful, and where it agrees with the patient will be of great service. Quinia administered in doses of two or three grains every two or three hours has been more effective and satisfactory in my practice than larger doses. I am of opinion that larger doses produce a kind of rigidity that interferes with the absorption of the agent, and consequently not so beneficial. Chlorate of potash in solution largely diluted, given alternately with quinia every one, two or three hours is a valuable agent. From one to two drams should be given daily—few remedies are better borne, and few restores the healthy hue of the blood as soon. Oxygen in these cases counts all the time; but the patients are almost always better after that. If these agents should disagree I would take the next best, and that would be the remedy or remedies that would agree best with the patient and accomplish the most for her benefit. If the patient improves and the unfavorble symptoms gradually yield, tonics will be proper. The elixir of calisaya, iron and bismuth is a favorite of mine, and has generally been satisfactory. Muriate tincture of iron, Fowlers solution and bichloride of mercury is another, but generally later in the course of treatment. Emulsion of cod liver oil is good. Cleanliness is important. Vaginal injections of tepid water will be proper, occasionally, but should in no way disturb the patient. Careful sponging the surface with tepid water or spirits and water, and as frequent changes of linen as the patient will bear are useful. The liver, kidneys and bowels need watching during the whole course of treatment, and such agents used as will keep the natural action in the different organs as near a healthy condition as possible. The bowels particularly should be regular. Coma is generally relieved by purgatives, stimulating applications along the spine and blisters to the nape of the neck.

Stimulants are generally required during the whole course of treatment, and should be used at such times and in such quantities as each individual case requires; wine, whiskey and brandy have their advocates. Whiskey I think best diluted with water or given in milk; others like wine or brandy. Which ever agent is used should be regulated to the condition of the patient; some require much more than others; there may be days or parts of days when stimulants will be all you have to depend upon; the amount required will depend on circumstances; from 8 to 50 ozs. daily; occasionally one will reject stimulants; generally there is not much hope for those cases; persons accustomed to their use in health will require heroic doses, but time and quantity must always be arranged to suit the patient and stage of the disease. Good nourishment well prepared and administered with prudence sums up the last point in the management of these kind of cases; bread is not always agreeable at first; milk, beef-tea, oysters, chicken broth, soup prepared from wild game if it can be procured, oat meal, farina, corn starch and perhaps eggs, coffee and tea if agreeable. While we are on the subject of nourishment, we should not forget that the digestive powers are defective from vitiated gastric secretion; administering nutriment alone will not build up and nourish a patient without agents to assist digestion; there is no class of patients more in need of pepsin or lactopeptine than the class we are now considering; one of these agents should always be administered after the food; this should never be forgotten.

Thomas More Madden, M. D. F. R. C. S. of the National Lying in Hospital, Dublin, Vol. 2, page 395, Ninth International Medical Congress, speaks of puerperal hygiene as an obvious method of diminishing puerperal septicæmia as follows. "For the prevention of puerperal septicæmia, the preparatory treatment of the patient before delivery by suitable nourishment, fresh air and appropriate tonics, is of primary importance. With this latter in view, I generally direct a mixture containing the chlorate of potash, iron and quinine, to be taken during a couple of months of gestation prior to her confinement, and I have never seen puerperal septi cæmia in a patient who had been thus treated before her confinement."

NERVOUS DISEASES.

There is no branch in the whole field of medical science and practice more extensive and complicated than diseases of the nervous system. When we examine the brain and spinal cord, the nervous system of animal life and the ganglionic or sympathetic the system of organic life, we can account for some of the phenomena in nervous affections. There we find the nervous system composed of two different substances, which differ from each other in density, color, in their minute structure and in their chemical composition. They are called the vesicular nervous matter and the fibrous nervous matter. The former is called the gray or cineritious substance, and the latter the white or medullary. The fibrous nervous matter is most extensively diffused throughout the body. It forms a large portion of the nervous centres, either alone or mixed with vesicular matter, and is the principle constituent of the nerves which connect them with the various tissues and organs. The vesicular matter is usually known by its soft consistence and dark reddish gray color; it is generally collected in masses intermingled with the fibrous structure in various parts of the brain and spinal cord, and in the several ganglia. The fibrous nervous matter consists of two different kinds of nerve fibres which are distinguished as the tubular fibre and the gelatinous fibre. In most nerves these two kinds are intermingled—the tubular fibres being more numerous in the nerves of the cerebro-spinal system; the gelatinous predominating in the nerves of the sympathetic system. The vesicular nervous substance is distinguished by its dark reddish gray color and soft consistence; it is found in the brain, spinal cord, and various ganglia intermingled with the fibrous nervous substance, but is never found in the nerves. The ganglia may be regarded as separate and independent nervous centres of smaller size and less complex structure than the brain; connected with each other, with the cerebro-spinal axis, and with nerves in various situations. The ganglia consist of the same elements as the other nerve centres: vesicular nervous matter, traversed by tubular and gelatinous nerve fibres. The corticle substance or gray matter is so thoroughly blended with the white matter, and the white fibres with the gray, that the combined influence of both are complete in all parts of the brain. In addition to the complete arrangement of the substance of the brain acting in harmony, we have a spinal cord closely connected with the brain and nervous system, and by these combined influences, through the nerves, will the organs of the body act in harmony. In the gray matter of the cord are cells with long processes: the origin of nerve roots. They are ganglionic in their nature and have the power of exciting motion and giving nutrition to the muscles. When disease attacks these ganglionic cells, paralysis of the muscles ensues, and wasting of the nerves. Placed laterally to the gray matter are the lateral columns: masses of nerve fibres passing along the cord, constantly receiving accessions from nerve roots, and in the upper part of medulla oblongata becomes the pyramidal tracts crossing over the opposite side and passing through the *pons caroli* into the peduncle, then upward direct with the cerebral tracts.

In the extreme borders of the anterior fissure in the white matter of the cord. They are white nerve fibres passing upward to the brain to conduct impressions from the brain. The difference between these nerve fibres is that the gray masses of nerve fibres cross over to the opposite brain hemisphere, and the white run direct to their own hemisphere. The anterior and posterior nerve roots pass out from the gray matter of the cord. The white matter in the region of the posterior roots is connected with sensation and co-ordination so that disease in this portion of the cord, their functions will be affected. There are nerve fibres passing out from the spinal cord into the sympathetic ganglia. Some of these fibres pass up from the cervical ganglia into the cranial cavity and to the vaso-motor nerves of the brain; others reach the eye and also to the heart and all the organs essential to life.

The conducting nerve fibres, both in the brain and in the spinal cord, and in the nerves themselves appear to have their nutrition regulated by certain ganglionic cells with which they are connected, so that when isolated from such cells they undergo degeneration. All functional acts are accompanied by or dependent upon nutritive changes. It matters not whether the functional act is connected with thought, consciousness or secretion, the generation of nerve force by the ganglionic cell and its transmission by the nerve fibre is accompanied by these nutritive changes in the body.

A nutritive act has a tendency to make an impression on

nerve tissue, and all nerve tissue is liable to be affected by its own functional actions. This applies equally to normal and to pathological actions; owing to this action, habits may be formed and become permanently impressed on the nervous system. The nutrition of the body depends upon the nutrition of the individual cells of which it is made up. Each cell has the power of appropriating from the blood such substances as will preserve its existence; enable it to perform its functions, and produce a successor; the cell is controlled by nerve power—even the nutrition of bone is influenced by the nervous system. When a bone is developing, a lesion of the nerve to it, or of the deeper portion of the spinal cord from which these nerves arise, will modify and partly arrest its growth. Each nerve has a connection with nerve cells from which it arises, and destruction of the cell, or division of its cylinder will produce degeneration of the nerve, and death of the part. Nerves do not coalesce, but pursue an uninterrupted course from the centre to the periphery; but do not pursue a perfectly insulated course, but occasionally join at a very acute angle with other branches running in the same direction, and from these branches others are given off, and this arrangement may extend for a considerable distance, and in no instance do they unite; but several branches may come together and form a plexus, and then increase their varied extensions. This arrangement gives the practitioner more trouble to find the true seat of disturbance.

A plexus is the communication between two or more nerves in their formation; the nerves may divide and join and subdivide. The branches passing off generally have more extensive connection with the spinal cord.

Location of lesions is to be arrived at by a knowledge of anatomy and physiology of the nervous system. In many cases under examination it is necessary for the physician to travel back from the symptoms to the cause of the disease, and study the family history—trace out predispositions, study the various causes of disease that the patient has been exposed to. In many cases the diagnosis may be found in causes outside of the nervous system, such as nodes, cicatrices, hemorrhage, renal disease, increased arterial tension, cerebral tuberculosis, pulmonary lesions, personal habits, over-work, self-abuse, tobacco, alcoholic beverages, injudicious diet, injurious employment, uraemia, anemia, malaria, punctured wounds, neuritis, brights disease, chronic diarrhœa, lithemia, heat; the altered condition of the nerves and organs after severe attacks of malignant fevers that pervert the functional activity of the nerve centres, and sometimes exist without the presence of any definite disease. Nerve exhaustion frequently takes place from the sedative effects of cold—slow, progressive sedation from cold will interfere with the reparative power of the system, and the cells will break down faster than new cells are formed. This condition of the system has confused and worried many physicians and families. Many physicians will imagine and guess at a variety of supposed causes, such as internal abscesses, tumors, brain disease, wasting of certain nerves, embolism, thrombosis and other conditions, before the true cause is discovered; and even a number of physicians are not willing to accept the true condition of the system when pointed out. This condition of the system, if fairly started, almost always ends fatally; the length of time depends largely on the original constitution and age of of the patient. Cold will bring on tetanus after wounds—even slight wounds that would not be troublesome if the patient was protected from the influence of cold. Excessive heat produces serious disturbance by its depressing influence in producing putrefactive changes in the fluids, and arrests respiration by paralyzing the respiratory centres. Dr. John Guituras recently in the navy reports a form of thermic fever in India and subtropical America almost identical in symptoms with the typhoid fever of the United States.

Fever is a disease that effects the whole system—it effects the head, trunk and extremities; it effects the circulation, absorption and the nervous system; it effects the skin, fibres, muscles and membranes; it effects the body, it effects the mind; it is therfeore a disease of the whole system in the fullest sense of the word. This explains why so many persons are nervous after attacks of fever, as all normal phenomena of the living organism are known to occur under the superintending influence of the nervous system, and are controlled by it; so it is but rational to regard all morbid actions as being more or less under the influence of the nervous system. Congestion is certainly the result of a peculiar disturbance in the nervous action. The nervous system is so delicate in its susceptibilities, and to the influences of the external world such as light, heat, moisture, electrical and toxic conditions, that changes are frequent and sometimes distressing; neither the strongest lenses of the microscope, nor the nicest analysis of chemistry have succeeded in discovering the faintest traces of the composition and character of these mysterious and stupendous agencies. We have no power over these agencies, but can try to fortify against their effects. There are reflexes of two kinds—superficial and deep; the first from nervous disturbance, from external irritations; the deep reflexes are from altered nerve structure beyond the surface, such as perforating ulcers, sphacelus, gangrene, even changes in the bones and joints, eye strain, diabetis, uramia, gastric, gouty, or other local troubles.

In considering palsies, it will be more satisfactory to divide the different kinds. First, general palsy, in which the whole muscular system is involved. It is of brain origin, and associated with symptoms of alteration of brain function. The lesion which produces it must affect both hemispheres of the brain; hemorrhage into both sides of the *pons varoli* will develope general palsy and severe apoplectic symptom.

Hemiplegia in which palsy affects one side of the body or at least the arm and leg of one side; this form of palsy is generally from a local brain lesion; sometimes, however, they may be of spinal origin, due to pressure of a tumor or wound in the upper section of the cord. If the attack comes on suddenly, it is generally by an embolus or thrombus, an abscess or tumor. If hemiplegia comes on slow, it is the result of an abscess localized cerebral softening of focal brain degeneration including tumors.

Paraplegia may come on in the course of two or three days, and when not connected with injury is due either to hemorrhage into the cord, or a hemorrhage into the vertebral canal outside of the cord; there are cases where injury is the cause of paralysis. In cases of gradual paraplegia with pain, they are disease of the vertebra or a growth usually sarcomatous or cancerous, situated to involve the nerves, or an aneurism pressing on the vertebra and nerves, may cause the trouble.

Monoplegia in which one member of the body is effected in the greater part of its muscular structure, and may be due to a lesion of the nerve or of the large multipolar cells in the anterior cornua of the spinal cord or of the brain cortex. In making the diagnosis in any case the general situation of the lesion is first to be determined.

Multiple palsies in which two or more disconnected district groups of muscles are paralyzed. The symptoms vary according to seat and nature of the lesion, and may be cerebral or periphery origin. There is one form of peripheral multiple palsy in which, although the muscle wastes, the reactions of degeneration do not appear. Local palsy in which a single muscle or a single group of muscles tributary to a single nerve is affected, and may be either centric or peripheral. The diagnosis of the nature of local palsy is to be made the same way of multiple palsies. Then we observe diseases in the brain and spine the very opposite of palsies—convulsions, chorea, spasms and tremors. In the convulsive form, we generally find divisions such as epilepsy, hysteria and tetanus. Epilepsy is a disease from organic disease of the brain, and the disease may be from different causes affecting the integrity of the brain and spinal cord; but the disease is more severe when the upper part of the brain is effected. Epilepsy may come on from poisons, toxaemia, uraemia or irritation transmitted to the brain to such a degree as to change the normal action of the organ.

The hysteroidal form is not generally so severe as to destroy life or impair the healthy action of the different organs, and in many cases will yield to treatment. Tetanus frequently starts from punctured wounds and peripheral irritation, and may be classed in the most severe and fatal forms of disease that the practitioner is called to treat.

Chorea starts from a diseased condition of the ganglionic structures of the cerebro-spinal axis and may exist without alteration of structure; sufficient to be determined by the microscope and if it continues long will generally be marked by structural changes; they are generally a lower tone of the nervous system than healthy nerve power, seldom met with in persons of robust nerve power.

Spasms, the reverse of paralysis, generally start from irritative lesions in the muscles and nerves.

Tremors are involuntary movements of the muscles and produced by different causes: in some cases they come on after excessive mental or physical work; in others from the excessive use of tobacco, coffee, tea or strong drink; then others from lead or mercurial poisoning, then the tremors of old age; and from multiple sclerosis of the brain. Tremors from sclerosis are suspended during sleep and repose. Charcot says that three-fourths of the cases of cerebro-spinal sclerosis, vertigo is present, and a whirling or revolving sensation is experienced.

Severe nerve trouble has occassionally followed blows and falls—the pia mater has been known to suffer after very slight injury and the small vessels in the corticle substance of the brain are frequently changed and in many cases microscopic examinations have revealed morbid changes scattered in different parts of the brain that was not visible to the eye. The gray substance is not fashioned in all parts of the encephalon upon the same model; there is a marked difference in different parts of the brain; and vascular ruptures thrombosis and emboli;

and even partial softening are sometimes found when they were not suspected. Prof. Sam'l Jackson was accustomed to say in his lectures at the University of Pennsylvania: "Whenever the expenditure of nerve force is greater than the daily income, physical bankruptcy sooner or later results." It is to be remembered that the nerve capital of persons differs almost as widely as does their moneyed capital. There are numerous families with very little nerve power from birth. Are born with less power of creating nervous energy than is necessary to meet the requirements of the ordinary duties of life.

There is every grade of natural nerve power; many persons are born with very little more nerve power than is necessary for breathing, eating and drinkink; and others have nerve power sufficient to enable them to bear incessant toil. This is frequently observed in the loss of life from very slight causes and indifferent wounds, and others would pass through the most malignant forms of disease and recover; and in many cases where they were riddled with bullets or terribly lacerated, would partially recover and live several years. In proportion to the supply of good healthy nerve power will the individual be able to perform the ordinary duties of life. Not one organ alone, but every organ of the body needs it, and must have healthy nerve influence or disease will be the result; and this supply must be regular night and day. Among civilized nations a perfectly healthy individual seems to be the exception rather than the rule. It is rare to meet a person at the age of thirty years who will not admit that at various times in their lives they have suffered from derangements of health in some form that the skillful physician can trace to disturbed action of the nervous system. It is not my intention to touch on the special senses such as sight, hearing, smell, taste and touch, or the mental and intellectual faculties generally. That would lead entirely beyond an ordinary paper. Each special sense would require a separate paper, and the same might be said of every organ in the body. I merely wished to examine a few forms of disease, that the general practitioner meets with in regular practice, associated more or less with the nervous system.

We have diseases of every kind and in every climate, many of them peculiar to certain localities and countries. But take the twenty-four hundred diseases mentioned, as found in the world, and a large proportion of them are of a nervous character; and let any disease exist in the human system long—the nervous system will be affected more or less, and when we take a grand survey of the world and all that effects man physically and mentally, we are ready then to acknowledge that he is fearfully and wonderfully made.

BACTERIA.

Bacteriology is occupying the attention of a great many scientific men on both continents, at the present time. Bacteria are defined at present to belong to the lowest organism of the vegetable kingdom, but their persistence and universality raised the question as to their origin and object. Investigation and observation led to the belief that they were capable of spontaneous generation and of fermentations, and a large number of virulent and contagious affections. The question as to the origin of life has been much disputed. The long ages of the past show the universality of the law of life, that like produces like. The germ theory asserts that no life has been evolved other than from a living parent or a living germ. Then again we find it disputed as whether bacteria ever occur in an animal in a perfectly healthy state. Some bacteria have only power of existence in tissue where vitality has entirely ceased, while others have power of existence in the presence of animal cells.

There are now over two hundred varieties known. I will not take the time necessary, at present, to refer to the different kinds mentioned by investigators, for there is a great discrepancy in the experiments made in different countries and by different persons. Many learned men claim that there are a specific bacilla that will always appear in a particular disease, and in no other, and that inoculations with pure cultures will always produce that disease. Others equally well qualified to test the effect of micro organisms on man, claim that the popular fear of bacteria is based on a misapprehension that the great mass of bacteria are innocent little bodies. They are known to exist in every country and climate, and almost every creature with life is loaded more or less with bacteria of some kind, without feeling any inconvenience when they are in a healthy condition.

Mequel found that the ordinary atmosphere of a large city contains over 2000 bacteria per cubic yard, and the air of a room of an old house in winter will show 4500 bacteria per cubic yard; the wards of a long used hospital as many as 90,000 germs in the same space; but all these germs must have soil for their development, and many of them powerless after one attack. When placed in a favorable condition they will double their numbers every hour. One bacterium will fill a half-pint measure in 48 hours, measuring 1-150000 of an inch each.

They are found in water—the water may appear clear, yet swarm with bacteria; nor does freezing lessen the danger of water; many bacteria are not affected by freezing. Nor do mineral springs remain free. A number of mineral springs in Europe have been examined and bacteria found in all of them.

Dr. Minges of Dubuque, Iowa, examined water taken from 19 mineral springs in the United States, and found bacteria more or less in all of them. Nor does elevation save mankind from bacteria. Culture mediums have been used to test localities; sterilized culture tubes have been prepared from blood serum. Agar, agar gelatine, meat infusion, peptone agar, liquid blood serum, veal broth, all sterilized by heat with cotton over the mouths of the tubes, and continued under the high temperature until every germ and spore was completely destroyed; then sealed over the cotton and taken carefully, carried to the

Alps, 7000 feet above sea level and opened, and in three days a number of them were swarming with bacteria; and the same tests have been used in our own country; they are found in the water at Fort Lewis in Southwest Colorado, 8000 feet above sea level, and in Montana at different places, ranging from 3,000 to 6,500 feet above sea level.

From the time of the first discovery of bacteria by Leewenhoeck, during his examination of saliva in 1675, bacteriology made no progress until about the middle of the present century. when Ehrenberg described several varieties, and Cohn classified them into bacilla micro cocci and spirilla; and in 1849 Pollender described rod like formations; and in 1863 Davaine undertook to prove a connection between bacteria and disease. Pasteur claimed some advances, and then Koch came forward and claimed to prove that wherever there is decomposition, bacteria are found; but in dry gangrene they are not found. Cutter speaks of Koch's bacilla as known thirty years ago; they were found in lager beer drips and in bread. Green's Pathology, page 41—"In necrosis, if the limb is much swollen, of a purplish color, and studded with bulla or blood stained fluid, and the part exposed to warm, moist air, septic bacteria will quickly enter through the skin and multiply rapidly." S. Weir Mitchell and Prof. Reichart experimented with rattlesnake poison, and found within an hour or two after an animal was bitten, the poison rots the vessels, and makes the blood fluid; then the system swarms with bacteria, connected with the putrefaction. If the venom is mixed with a strong solution of potassa or soda its power is killed; permanganate of potash is the best agent. There are certain localities where many of the severe forms of disease are not found although Koch, Tyndell, Atkin and Mcquel have proved to the world the existence of microbes in houses, and in the open air. Dengue seldom spreads in localities over 2000 feet above sea level. Savannah, Georgia, with surroundings similar to other southern cities; the water supply is from surface wells, river water, driven wells and artesian wells, and hydrophobia, puerperal fever, typhus fever and vesical calculous diseases are unknown. Typhoid fever, cholera and cerebro-spinal meningitis has died out. Erysipelas, sun-stroke, croup and renal calculi are rarely met with; diphtheria and cholera infantum and exanthematus diseases very mild; yellow fever and dengue at long intervals; malarial diseases very much modified. Gastro-intestinal disorders and diseases of the lungs are the common diseases met with, and are very frequent.

Surgeon Sternberg, after a stay of six months in Cuba studying the cause of yellow fever, has failed to find a specific microbe described by Dr. Friere of Brazil, or the microbe of Koch in cholera, not even in the cadaver. In the year 1873 cholera, cerebro-spinal meningitis, small pox, yellow fever, bilious fever, congestive fever, dengue, gastric fever, intermittent, malarial, remittent, nervous fever, puerperal fever, scarlet fever, typhoid and typhus fevers all prevailed at the same time in New Orleans. And in 1887 typhoid fever and diphtheria prevailed at the same time in the same city. In the cases of diphtheria the bacilla found in the false membranes were not discoverable in the lymphatic glands, in the blood or the viscera. The bacilla in many cases produced the disease in guinea pigs and rabbits, but not in rats or mice. In all cases the cultures lost their toxic powers when boiled.

Flugge states that his experiments with both the dejections and inoculations with pure cultures of the typhoid bacilla was always successful. Vaughan, Eberth, Koch, Gaffky, Frankel, Simonds, Seits and others who investigated typhoid fever patients for the typhoid bacilla, failed in many cases. All the experiments made by Murchison, Klein and Bahredt with typhoid stools and with the blood of typhoid patients by inoculation were without success. Novy experimented with the drinking water of the Iron mountain, Michigan, where there was a severe epidemic of typhoid fever with negative results. From all we can obtain we have good reason for regarding typhoid fever as due to mixed infection, as the majority of investigators in search of the typhoid bacilla are compelled to give the so-called germ a secondary role in the greater number of their cases in that disease. Profs. Wood and Flint taught that well-marked cases of typhoid fever rarely exist where malarial fevers prevail.

The antagonism between the malarial poison and the cause of typhoid has been observed for many years. Malarial poison rapidly destroyes the colored corpuscles of the blood. This direct solution of the problem of the poisonous properties of the stagnent waters of the swamps, marshes and rice fields introduced into the blood of the inhabitants explains the origin of intermittent, remittent, congestive and pernicious fevers, and other forms of malignant diseases. When the water was boiled or distilled for domestic use the malarial diseases diminished. The blood was always diseased first. A number of recent experimenters are of opinion that the bacilla of tuberculosis is of the nature of a fungous, and requires for its growth a soil in which organic decay is taking place in tissue of very low vitality prone to break down.

The ptomaines are artificial alkaloids found in decomposing animal matter when dead. Leucomaines are artificial alkaloids in living matter; in healthy conditions they do no harm, but in disease they may enter the morbid structure and increase the virulence of the disease in the modified animal tissue in many cases. The best treatment is change of climate, hygiene and good nutrition. Dr. Pepper believes that in all infectious diseases from scarlet fever to tuberculosis it is a question both of the soil and specific poison; and the symptoms and course of the disease, and not simply the life history of the microbe; but they are the expression of the reaction of the system and of the secondary disturbances of function. Dr. Richardson of London, thinks it a great mistake to assume the infective action of a microbe in consumption. He repeats, consumption seems to indicate an hereditary diathesis; an hereditary failure of nutrition, and upon this the bacilla tuberculosis becomes engrafted. The experiments of Dr. Cutter led him to believe that consumption was brought on from the spores of vinegar yeast in the blood, which by their size and chemical action produced tubercle. He found in tuberculosis the blood was sticky and ropy masses of red corpuscles saturated with spores of vinegar yeast, and also vinegar yeast spores in the serum, and when vinegar yeast was detained in the lungs, tubercle was formed. This yeast comes from the bowels and is produced by the fermentation of starches and sugar; and so long as there are masses of vinegar yeast in the blood the patient is in danger of lung necrosis. When the blood becomes healthy, then nature has a chance to heal the lung.

The bacteriologists of the present day are willing to admit that there are only a few specific bacteria that are to be dreaded, and that the human organism is not affected by the larger number of the microbes, for they are satisfied that a large portion of our food is filled with microbes—particularly milk. There have been 18 different varieties of bacilla found in the alimentary canal of milk fed infants, without impairing the health, and that the bacilla found in one form of disease destroys the bacilla in other forms of disease; and in many diseases there are no bacilla found.

Doctors Hunt of New Jersey, Plater of Canada and Kretchman of Brooklyn, on the indiscriminate and promiscuous expectoration of the victims of consumption on the floor or pavement, that when the expectoration has dried by the atmosphere, some individuals will present a suitable soil for its development. They believe the best means of protection against germ diseases is to be found in so maintaining the general condition of the body, that it will resist the action of the germs, even should they find access thereto. That where there is a tendency in an individual to pulmonary disease, they should never engage in any indoor occupation, and should exercise the lungs frequently by deep and prolonged inspirations and expirations in the open air.

In all their investigations connected with pulmonary disease, where germs were found, they found a soil congenial for their development. They have shown that in many cases of tuberculosis, bacteria disappeared entirely from the lungs; yet the disease progressed and resulted in death. Rossi of Rome, found bacteria in the follicles of the tonsils in healthy men and in the saliva, and caused no harm.

Doctors Straus and Murtz experimented with gastric juice on the bacilla of tubercle, charbon, typhoid fever and cholera morbus. The gastric juice of man, of dogs and of sheep were selected for the experiment. They found that for a few hours digestion at a temperature of 100 degrees destroyed all the germs. The bacilla of anthrax was killed in half an hour; the bacilla of typhoid and cholera in less than three hours; but the bacilla of tubercle bore digestion for six hours, and in some cases up to 12 hours—over 12 hours digestion destroyed it completely; they believed it was the acid that was the true germicide, for they found hydro-chloric acid diluted with water in the same proportion as it is in the gastric juice proved as active a destroyer of the bacilla. Pepsin had no influence on the germs.

They are of opinion that the germs taken into the stomach during ordinary nutrition are not exposed to the acid constituents of the gastric juice so direct and prolonged action as in the experiments. Very thorough experiments have been carried on with germicides, with a view to ascertaining the smallest quantity of any antiseptic substance which is capable of preventing the development of the bacilla of typhoid fever, cholera and tuberculosis. The culture of the typhoid bacilla was prevented by one part of corrosive sublimate on 20,000 parts of culture medium; one part of sulphate of quinia on 800 parts of culture medium, and one part of carbolic acid on 200; one part of hydrochloric acid on 105 parts; and one part of chloride of lime on 100 parts of culture medium. Koch tells us that the cholera bacilla will not develop in an acid medium; one drop of a 1 per cent. solution of hydro-chloric acid prevents it. The cholera bacilla is prevented by one part of corrosive sublimate on 100,000 parts of culture medium; one part of sulphate of quinia on 5000, one part of sulphate of copper on 500 parts, and one part of carbolic acid on 400 parts of culture medium. And silicate of soda, polysulphide of potassium, fluo silicate of iron, salycilic acid and ammonia will sterilize the culture mediums of tubercular bacilla.

A temperature of 132 degrees will destroy the bacilla of authrax, typhoid fever, glanders, cholera, erysipelas, vaccinia, rinderpest and sheep pox. The cholera germ yellow fever germs, scarlet fever and small pox germs do not form spores. A temperature of 212 degress for one and a half hours will destroy bacteria without spores; a temperature of 284 degrees F. will destroy spores in 3 hours. Dr. A. M. Bell, of New York, has tested steam He says steam at a temperature of 220° F for ten minutes or 145° for two hours is fatal to all known germs of disease. Mercuric chloride 1 part in 1000 will destroy all spores in a few minutes; it is better than carbolic acid.

It is generally agreed that bacteria belongs to the vegetable kingdom, and if these microbes were capable of producing their special form of disease every time we are brought in contact with them there would be no chance for any of us to live.

Now we will very briefly show that the opinions of the bacteriologists at the present day will not bear them out, when compared with the wisdom and experience of the best men in the medical profession in all ages and in all countries. Take for example the microbes found in osteo myelitis and inject them into another person--you will not find the same disease produced. And the same way with endo-carditis. Take a case of small pox, and the individual may be young when the disease was contracted, and after recovery may be surrounded with variola microbes for three score years and no more disease of that kind. Why is it so? If these bacilla are so dangerous, and there are many instances where persons come in contact with variola many times during life and never had the disease, there was no soil there for the bacilla. Take yellow fever, and very few have second attacks; and many not at all; there is no diseased tissue there. Take typhoid fever, scarlet fever, cholera and let us go down along the line of tho diseases supposed to be brought about by bacteria, and we find them living and enjoying good health for three score years and ten, surrounded by millions of microbes supposed to be generators of diseases, all the days of their lives. Very frequently persons are taken away with pulmonary consumption without any microbes about the system. The parasitical experience comes from the laboratory, and are very different from the living organism. We are told that bichloride of mercury will kill all forms of parasites. Why not cure pulmonary consumption and all forms of contagious and dangerous diseases with the remedy.

How can the bacteriologist assert that there are certain microbes that will kill a human being in a short time, and then acknowledge that there are several kinds in many diseases, and cannot possibly tell which one is really the most dangerous in certain diseases; and where there is a well developed disease in the system, to kill the microbes would kill the patient, and with the next breath acknowledge that we ordinarily take in millions in a few hours in the water we drink, the bread we eat and the air we breathe, and still continue in the best of health? We see from all the progress made in the different experimental methods that they are nothing less than hypothesis and systematic tendencies—they are very far from perfection. Many physicians when blinded by a hobby try to find good reasons to console themselves for their non-success. The existence of some of the recent ideas have wrought a condition in their brains as disastrous as the bacilla in the lungs of their patients. Within a few years we had Bergeon's gas treatment, Pasteurism, then came Brown Seguard's elixir of life; they have gone the way of all the earth. I hope they are happy. And last but not least, Koch's lymph. If we look straight forward we can see the hand writing on the wall in different languages, giving all nations, kindreds and tongues warning that the same host is hastening back to remove the last great failure from the face of the earth.

There is an harmonious agreement between ancient and modern observers that hereditary predispositions exist; and they also agree that good hygienic conditions—pure air, good nourishment and everything that will augment the vitality of the cells and invigorate the whole system—will cripple the tendency to disease, and defy microbes. What we have said concerning hereditary diseases will hold good in many other diseases. If the soil is wanting, the disease will not be modified by microbes.

The true physician must drop experimental empiricism and follow the great truths of clinical observations and scientific medicine furnished by the bright lamp of physics, of chemistry, of physiology and of pathological anatomy.

TOBACCO.

Tobacco is an annual plant with a large fibrous root, rising from three to six feet high; the lower leaves are often two feet long and six inches broad. The original locality of tobacco is not well settled. The Spaniards found it in tropical America; the Chinese claim that it was cultivated in Asia, before Columbus discovered America. In the early writings of Dr. Benjamin Franklin he refers to Indian traditions, claiming that tobacco was given to the six nations; and central Pennsylvania near the Susquehanna river was the place the first tobacco grew, and that the Spaniards obtained it from the American Indians, and introduced it into their country in 1518. History mentions the introduction of tobacco into France in 1560, into Holland in 1615, into England in 1665, and into China about the same time. After its introduction into Europe there were efforts made to suppress its use. Physicians declared it hurtful to health, the priests denounced its use as sinful; snuff was prohibited in churches; the Sultan of Turkey was in favor of making the use a capital offense; in Russia the nose was to be mutilated if used. James 1 of England declared it loathsome to the eye, hurtful to the nose, hurtful to the brain and dangerous to the lungs; but still the habit in all its vile forms went on, destroying body and mind. Let us look at the authorities as recorded in the United States Dispensatory and the National Dispensatory, the precipitate of the wisdom of all observers, of all experimenters of all ages, in all countries, giving the properties and the effects of tobacco. These statements are made as follows: "Tobacco is a powerful sedative poison, and locally irritant and hostile to all forms of life. Plants confined in rooms where snuff is manufactured soon lose their foliage; nearly all insects shun tobacco. Tobacco owes its poisonous properties to the presence of a liquid volatile, alkaloid, nicotine or nicotina; this is a deadly poison, and like prussic acid destroys life in small doses with great rapidity." A child three years of age died from using an old wooden pipe to blow soap bubbles.

"There is 4 per cent. of nicotine in tobacco smoke. Nicotine acts poisonously upon all animals, even on frogs and snakes. The blood of a person during life, if examined when under the full influence of tobacco, presents a striking disintegration of the red corpuscles of the blood, which are less regularly circular than natural. It lessens the natural appetite, and more or less impairs digestion and induces constipation; irritates the mouth and throat, rendering regular congestion, and destroying the purity of the voice. It induces an habitual sense of uneasiness and nervousness, with epigastric sinking or tension-palpitation and neuralgia. Chewing and snuffing cause gastralgia, and smoking neuralgia of the fifth pair of nerves. It renders the vision weak and uncertain and sometimes amaurosis; also the hearing suffers with ringing and buzzing in the ears. It impairs muscular power, nutrition and sleep, and also the nerve force. A few may not experience the general effects above mentioned, but the greater number addicted to the habit will experience the injurious effects, and in a certain number of cases it acts in almost all doses as a poison."

Let us look at the testimony we have from facts laid before the International Medical Congress in 1887, Vol. 4, page 101: "Chronic pharyngitis is one of the common results from chewing and smoking tobacco, and many cases of the so-called clergyman's sore throat is nothing more nor less than a tobacco throat. Smoking tobacco is a great injury to the air passages, producing irritation of the mucous membrane lining the trachea and larger bronchial tubes, which finally results in chronic inflammation of the parts irritated. In many cases the nasal mucous membrane, the epiglottis and true vocal cords are kept in a highly congested state. Throats in this condition are always aggravated by exercise and prolonged use of the voice. Persons suffering with the irritation produced by tobacco are always slow in recovering from acute inflammatory diseases of the air passages. The practice called dipping is the very worst form to use tobacco; it is inhaled in a finely comminuted state; where there is a tendency to pulmonary disease, it will hasten a fatal termination, and the eyes are known to be effected by the habit; more particularly amblyopia and diseases of the cheeks."

Let us look into Taylor's Medical Jurisprudence, page 253. This work is a standard authority on poisons, recognized by our courts and medical profession throughout the United States and England:

"The effects of tobacco when taken in large doses either in powder or infusion, are as follows: The symptoms are faintness, nausea, vomiting, giddiness, delirium, loss of power in the limbs, general relaxation of the muscular system, trembling, complete prostration of strength, coldness of surface, with cold, clammy perspiration, convulsive movements, paralysis and death." In some cases, violent pain in the abdomen; in others sinking or depression in the region of the heart. Tobacco operates as a poison when applied externally. A woman aged 40, suffering from varicose veins, struck her leg accidently against a sewing machine; severe hemorrhage followed; to stop this she applied tobacco to the wounds. In a short time there were alarming symptoms; a physician was called in, the tobacco was removed, and stimulants administered, and the woman recovered.

When we study the effects of tobacco and fail to discover any benefit in any part of the world or for any useful purpose whatever, we have the right to ask the question: What is it raised for? The annual production of tobacco in all countries is about 3,000,000 tons. In 1875 there were 559,000 acres planted in the United States, yielding 367,000,000 pounds of tobacco. Only two reasons can be given for this immense production: the first is the revenue—the internal revenue from the sale of tobacco in every form in the United States, for the year 1890, was $33,958,991; and the other is to dwarf the human family in body, mind and soul—to destroy one-tenth of their happiness and one-fifth of their lives. Many will tell you "I don't use much, I can quit it any time," but the experience of the world proves that the use of narcotics and stimulants continued for a time leads to habit, and when habit is formed it is seldom, or with great difficulty, overcome.

It is not doubted that tobacco contains poisonous principles which possess the power of arresting the oxidation of living tissues, most deleterious to the young, causing in them impairment of growth, premature manhood and physical degredation.

The cigarette is a small cigar wrapped in paper; the best wrappers are made in Switzerland, from rice straw. Their manufacture is nearly new in the United States; the extensive use of the article is recent here. Cigar stumps are frequently used along with leaves to manufacture them. A cigarette is so small that it looks harmless, but it contains more poison than a cigar; the smoke from the paper wrappings sends more poisonous fumes into the lungs than a pipe or a cigar. An ordinary cigarette contains nicotine enough to kill two men if taken pure. There is all the way from three to seven pounds of nicotine in a hundred pounds of tobacco—one drop of nicotine placed on the tongue of a dog will instantly kill the animal. The use of cigarettes brings on tremor, palpitation, and tendency to paralysis and many serious forms of disease.

Another effect of tobacco in the world is the intemperate use of spiritous, vinous, brewed and malt liquors. It is the forerunner of drunkenness. Let us take the drunkard's infancy, early life, youth, manhood and old age in all its horrors, with every link and step, and the tobacco evil shows its hideous face all along the line. Take the sons of the chewer and smoker, and you see the effects of indigestion, depressed nerve power, vitiated secretion, insensibility to all the higher and nobler feelings of humanity transmitted to their offspring. These unfortunates seek something at an early age to gratify and satisfy their tainted organisms. What do they seek? Whiskey, opium, chloral or coca.

Many years ago I was requested by an aged gentleman of more than ordinary qualifications and opportunities to observe and study the families of Indiana county. (Dr. James M. Stewart.) He remarked to me "I have watched the rising generation in our country around us for 40 years, and in almost every case where I saw a boy using tobacco at 10 years of age, I saw a drunkard at 25, and since that time I have observed many so-called temperance men in our county, active in temperance societies, who would not touch strong drink nor permit it to be kept about their houses, but at the same time were slaves to the tobacco habit; and their children were nearly all fond of strong drink.

At an early period in our county there were a great many small distilleries. I can take you to places where 40 different distilleries stood in Indiana county, and very little drunkenness at that period; and what appears remarkable, the boys raised where whiskey was manufactured, were generally the most temperate men in our county—very few exceptions. At a later date, many years after they left the distilleries and commenced to use tobacco, some of these persons became intemperate. When we are on the subject of intoxicating drinks we may as well give the true cause of so much intemperance, with the horrid degredation and all accompanying evils connected with the traffic.

First, the hereditary appetite. Second, patent medicines in the form of cordials and soothing syrups poured into children when they are young, and in some cases for many years; and I have several times noticed two or three old pipes started in rooms where there were infants not more than one hour old. After they are smoked, and dosed on patent medicine for a few years, they are ready for something stronger. These patent remedies prepared for children are composed largely of sedatives and narcotics; then candy and all the truck sold at such places—the morbid taste cultivated by the use of the confectionery stock, prepares them in a short time for tobacco, then whiskey, then the drunkard preceding the drunkard's grave, with all its consequences. The whiskey vender does not make the drunkard. He sells to the drunkard after he is a drunkard. The tobacconist and whiskey vender will look at you with a saintly countenance and say: "I ask no one to buy." But there are purchasers all the same when the articles are before the public, and advertised for sale.

If the young were protected and properly trained and all the old sinners were led into a decent form of living, and treated tobacco as the greatest curse visible on the face of the earth, then the fearful consequences would be avoided. Go back and read its properties and effects as I have shown you from the highest authorities, and you will see that it curses everything it touches.

Take the animal that walks on all four—even the swine that the evil spirits chose to ride into the sea, will not degrade themselves with the weed; and the serpents, the copperhead and rattlesnake, will not chew nor suck the weed.

Now I will refer very briefly to two important duties devolving on every human being. After God had made all other creatures he said let us make man in our image, after our likeness; and requires all lawful endeavors to preserve our own lives and the lives of others, and forbiddeth the taking away of our own lives or the life of our neighbor, or whatsoever tendeth thereunto. The first duty may be considered under the head of hygiene.

Hygiene is the art of preserving health; that is, of obtaining the most action of body and mind during as long a period as is consistent with the laws of life. In other words, it aims at rendering growth more perfect, decay less rapid, life more vigorous and death more remote. The use of tobacco is positively in opposition to hygiene. If no one would touch tobacco how long would it be raised and offered for sale? If no one would use intoxicating drinks as a beverage, how many saloons and licensed bars would be in the land.

In the second duty we are bound to the following applications: We are commanded to "be pure in body and mind," and as we have opportunity we ought to "do good to all men," and "train up children in the way they should go, and when they are old they will not depart from it;" and to "love thy neighbor as thyself," for "what a man soweth, that shall he also reap;" "he that is filthy shall be filthy still." And when the second division of the great and innumerable host appears at the resurrection, it will be found that tobacco and patent medicines are not the least offenses charged against their friends in this life.

HYGIENE.

[Thesis submitted to the faculty of the Jefferson Medical College, Philadelphia, Pa., December, 1851:]

For the support and nourishment of the system of man, it

HYGIENE. 179

is necessary for the different organs to be in a healthy condition; without this, no one can enjoy the rich blessings of health for a great length of time. When disease attacks the different organs of the body, though small at the commencement, it will eventually break in on the various connections in the human system, still opening a wider road for the ravages of the morbid condition, until at last it deranges that beautiful structure in its wondrous forms.

For the proper performance of Hygiene, many points present themselves for consideration. We have nothing of more importance in the protection of health, than the inhalation of pure air into the lungs. A well ventilated apartment is a useful adjuvant to the remedies we apply in the treatment of disease. As soon as the infant enters the world, the air rushes into its lungs, the circulation of the blood through that organ commences, and from that moment life depends very much on the air that is inhaled into the nostrils, which is incessantly taken in and thrown out of the lungs, hence the necessity of having constantly a renewed supply of pure atmosphere. As a portion of the atmospheric air is frequently corrupted by the respiration of men and animals, by the burning of so many natural and artificial fires, by the dissolution and putrefaction of innumerable substances, which if inhaled for a length of time, renders the system unfit for its many duties.

This property so important to life, is much improved by light and heat from the sun, which has a very efficacious tendency in counteracting the baneful effects of corruption and putrefaction. This we believe to be the cause of many of the diseases existing throughout the land, appearing in various forms in different localities, commencing in the most fertile plains, finding its way over mountains and through valleys, carrying with it the features of a malarious disease in one place, in another appearing in a modified form; but still growing sufficiently to convince us of its nature; and we are unable to form a correct knowledge of the manner in which it attacks the system of many. Nothing has been discovered to satisfy as to its peculiar nature—creeping in as it were by magic, until it prostrates the whole structure; sometimes the seeds lying dormant in the system for weeks or months, until they are roused by some indisposition, when they spring forth with as much force as if sown recently.

No doubt the surface is often affected by miasmatic influences, especially where we are under an unfavorable atmosphere. The numerous contaminations acting as foreign substances on the body, checking the free, full and healthful condition of the surface, causing determinations to internal organs, keeping up local congestions, acute and chronic inflammations, producing many irregularities and obstructions, between the various organs on which our health depends, and disease is the result. To remedy this cause, we must protect ourselves against the changes of the seasons, and ward off whatever presents itself in the form of miasm. If we are not able to protect ourselves against such attacks, by our remedial agents, we must change our location, where the atmosphere will be more favorable to the circulation, keeping up the vital force in every organ, securing the necessary stimulus to the endangium for the support and nourishment of the blood, enabling every organ to perform its function—preventing the decomposition of the material so essential to life; this keeps the nervous power in operation, and by it every tissue is sustained with power sufficient to perform its duty, driving the consumed particles into the pores, where they are conveyed out of the body, through the different channels, when in a healthy condition. When this process is retarded, the system is changed in some part, a laxity of the tissues is brought on, which leads to weakness or perversion of function, so that instead of a sufficient quantity of well elaborated material, for the purposes of nutrition, there is separated from the blood a peculiar product of the lowest grade of vital force, with a tendency to degeneration fixed upon it, which exists as a foreign matter in the midst of living structures, perverting the vital forces below the healthy standard, sometimes even to extreme debility.

Amongst the many points of consideration for the judicious course in preserving health, is proper attention to food. The first of our articles of diet is that food which we receive from our mother's bosom. Nature is furnished with aliment to satisfy the hunger and thirst of the infant. When taken into the stomach in large quantities, it is too much distended, and by degrees acquires an unnatural craving for food, which must be satisfied whatever be the consequence. These excessive supplies not only produce serious and fatal disorders, but also retard the growth, and eventually diminish the digestive power of the stomach. If we use for some time a good selection of articles, the stomach becomes so habituated to them that we feel indisposed as soon as we transgress, and the digestive power soon becomes impaired. People in health require no excitement to relish good and wholesome food—the simple dish is the most palatable.

Attention is necessary to peculiar constitutions. Such a selection of animal and vegetable food as proves to be nourishing and easy of digestion is the proper regimen for the healthy economy. Regular periods, as well as the food being received gradually into the stomach, as it is duly prepared by mastication. The mode of preparation is often the cause of disease; if this department was carefully attended to, health would be promoted—at least better prepared for the toils and changes of life.

When food is properly masticated and has received a sufficient quantity of saliva, it is prepared for passing into the stomach, where it is acted on by the gastric juice as well as the churning action of that organ. If there is too great a quantity of fluids taken into the stomach, it prevents the ordinary course of digestion by causing the organ to perform a greater amount of labor than it is accustomed to, though a proper share of fluid is necessary for the performance of digestion.

Drinks ought always to be taken in moderate quantities; these should be pure and of the most simple kind—an undue proportion of drink renders the mass of the blood too thin, and occasions a general debility of constitution. Stimulating fluids should be avoided, as they are apt to bring on an unusual degree of excitement—affect the nerves and leave a state of depression which weakens the digestive powers. The process of mastication, insalivation, and deglutition are important, not only for preparing the food for the gastric juice, but allowing proper time for the stomach to act on a mere morsel as it passes into it, and by this course it is not injured by too rapid distention. After this gradual and moderate action, the chyme is pure, and all the secretions are sufficient to meet the demands of the various organs of the body.

If the bulk and quality in the articles of diet contain sufficient aliment, the sensibility and muscular contractions are directed to the process of digestion; when the chyme is formed it passes into the duodenum, where it receives the different secretions, preparing chyle to be taken up through the proper channel for the nourishment and support of the various organs of the body, after which separation the healthy condition of the body requires an evacuation of all the excrementitious matter remaining in the bowels. If the individual is enjoying good health there is generally no difficulty produced in the course of nature. Should there be any failure in regular evacuations, the system is likely to suffer; remedies for this object should be resorted to, and the individual instructed as to the best articles of regimen, and the formation of regular habits. Some attention should be paid to animal and vegetable substances, as digestion is very much facilitated by tenderness of fibre and minute divisions of the various substances.

The structure of the system is calculated for the performance of a great amount of exercise. It is necessary for every able bodied person to be engaged in some employment, for the preservation of health, as inactivity never fails to induce a relaxation of the contractile fibres, and when the fibres are relaxed, neither digestion nor circulation can be duly performed, though sedentary employments may be mixed with a due quantity of exercise and not injure health. The exercise should be daily and regular, and by all means in the open air, that the human frame may receive that bracing and strengthening power designed for it by the Creator, to ward off disease.

If the different emunctories are obstructed and the many crude and acrid substances retained, nature must suffer in proportion to the malignity and duration of the offending matter. Frequently nature is compelled to relieve herself by more unusual channels, such as bleeding at the nose in plethoric young people; hemorrhoids in others (generally in those more advanced in life;) sometimes ulcers arise in those individuals whose fluids are in an impure state. The saliva may become very profuse, and great mischief may be done to individuals by these conditions.

Proper attention to cleanliness is one of the safest remedies to counteract fatal effects; it may be considered the grand secret of preserving beauty, as well as promoting health. All ages and sexes are alike applicable to its benefits; the softness of the skin is maintained, the limbs are pliant, the complexion gives evidence of purity; the whole constitution is kept bright and in full vigor. By frequent ablutions impurities are thrown off, cutaneous obstructions removed, and the surface is preserved and many threatening disorders are prevented. It soon attracts our regard and becomes agreeable to our nature. It does not only adorn us with a virtue, that we can go into company without giving offense, but preserves many of the higher passions of the mind, not only making us agreeable to others, but easy to ourselves; promoting health of body and mind, so that pure and unsullied thoughts are naturally suggested to the mind by those objects that perpetually encompass us, when they are beautiful and elegant in their kind. Our senses are governed more by refined feelings, and inlets made to reason.

We may now with propriety notice the effects of intemperance. The mind that is fortified by temperance leads to health and happiness. If anything is used in excess, pain and misery is the result; it is necessary in all things to be cautious, especially in our meat and drink. If we destroy a healthy constitution by intemperance, knowingly, we do as manifestly kill ourselves as though we were to hang ourselves with a rope, or to take poison sufficient to put an end to our existence. Our desires should be regulated, so that we may enjoy every pleasure with moderation. Voluptuousness should never be suffered to overcome us. Our relish is much diminished by excesses. The intoxicating draught is undoubtedly the most miserable refuge for misfortune; the result of it is short life, sinking spirits; one dose opening the way for another, until the miserable man falls a slave to the draught and becomes a sottish sacrifice. Let those who taste, remember that custom changes into habit, and habit soon becomes a second nature, very difficult to be subdued. Little unsuspecting beginnings generally contract vice, and seldom terminate but with life. Every pleasure that is pursued to excess converts itself into destruction.

If the monuments of death were read, we would have a more instructive lecture on moderation than any of the most eloquent writers can give. Behold the graves peopled with the victims of intemperance; view the chambers of darkness hung round on every side with the trophies of luxury, drunkenness and sensuality. As it has been asserted, "Where war or pestilence have slain their thousands, intemperate pleasure has slain its ten thousands.

The healthy economy may be much assisted by clothing. We must dress according to our situations. The great object of clothing of different kinds is to keep the body warm and uniform. This valuable shield to the comfort of mankind is often abused by the imprudent. There appears to be a transcendant faculty of reason, wisely left with man to accommodate himself with clothing to suit the different climates and seasons. Clothing alone will not entirely protect us from the fatal effects occasioned by the sudden changes of our climate, yet by a good selection we may avoid much danger. Such clothing should be worn as will maintain a comfortable temperature of the surface, so as to prevent a profuse perspiration and bring on debility. The surface should be clean and dry, the clothing frequently changed, and above all precautions the clothing ought to be dry; this applies to our couch as well as our every day garment. We should not be overloaded with clothes so as to heat the blood more than is consistent with health, producing copious exhalations which weaken the organs relaxed by sleep. This rest is the great restorer of nature, introduced as a welcome vacation for both the body and soul. The health and happiness of mankind depends greatly on a due amount of sleep; without this accustomed repose the whole frame is in a short time thrown into disorder, the appetite is impaired, the mind is partially abridged and the spirits dejected; the body sinks gradually into a state of inactivity; the blood circulates slowly, perspiration is disordered; the memory becomes feeble, and sensibility is in a great measure destroyed; but where a proper share of this reviving rest is obtained, the feeble brain and hands repair their exhausted vigor, many of the pensive thoughts drop their load of sorrows, and the busy ones rest from the fatigue of application.

The great Author of nature draws around us the curtain of darkness, which conceals everything that disturbs the senses and favors the inclination to drowsiness and repose, which rouses the weary frame from its exhaustion, and prepares us for the many arduous duties of life; for the mind needs to be refreshed constantly. If the mind should be agitated it has a tendency to diminish the powers of the body, enfeebling the nervous system and opening the way for many complaints. It is of the highest importance to avoid all rigorous excitement; we are too apt to yield to slight provocations, which produces a nervous tremor, increases the circulation; every nerve and muscle is brought into action, and often over-exerted by violence, and is compelled to give way sooner or later, leaving a state of depression, very uncomfortable, and frequently dangerous. Local disorders may arise from the extreme exertion occasioned by the excitement, and if exposed to contagion, the virus may enter the system, seize the opportunity of developing itself in the different organs during the depressed condition, making inroads to the very centre, exposing the system to all the ravages of disease.

A little caution would no doubt save many dangerous and fatal disorders. Distress brought on by envy or malice generally rivets on the mind a corrosive poison, which frequently destroys all rest and torments until all the more agreeable feelings are corrupted, imbibing prejudice and envy until the malicious intention is heightened in its malignancy; breaking down all pure and refined feelings, leaving the person an enemy to all around him; a disgrace to his friends; restless and full of terror to himself, his mind leading onward and downward until his days are days of trouble, and his existence difficult to be borne.

We should be careful to avoid violent passions, attended with so much evil, causing us to be unpleasant to our companions and uncomfortable to ourselves. It destroys many of the powers of doing good, injures our health and plunges us into disgrace. A little well directed prudence would no doubt keep us in the limits of moderation, and have the confidence of all around. We would not be likely to neglect our business, destroy our health and bring on poverty and disgrace. The evil does not stop here. It is truly lamentable that we live in an age in which many of the qualities and conditions are excessively addicted to vice, and it must be fresh in the memory that many of the most atrocious deeds have been committed, whilst under the influence of a violent passion. We are flattered by the subtle invader until we are tarnished with disgrace and compelled to blush at our actions.

Our minds should be cultivated so as not to be led into extremes. It appears that people possessed of great fortitude are not so readily infected by contagious disorders, as those more timid. Many persons under a violent fit of fear contract disease on entering the chamber of the sick once or twice. The mind should be preserved so as not to be suddenly surprised when calamities and afflictions befall us; it should be preserved in ease and serenity. The best remedy against a torturing state of the mind is a good conscience, which is to the soul what health is to the body. It is this that keeps our hearts from bursting under the pressure of evils and calamities; it caresses us in all extremes and gives the unhappy an expectation of happiness in the bosom of futurity. The mind has a great influence on the state and disorders of the body; if we can call to our assistance the strong powers of the mind, it proves of great service to the mechanical operation of drugs; if we can obtain the desired imagination, it presently makes some impression in the brain, whence proceeds a motion of the sensitive soul and of the spirits that excite the passion of hope. By it, the activity of the whole machine is enlivened, the action of the heart and arteries is increased, the circulation of all the fluids is more vigorous and uniform, preventing the formation of disease, and facilitating the cure of such as are formed. The body should be prepared to gradually undergo the emotion connected with it.

We must be fortified with a necessary share of firmness to meet joyful tidings, as well as disastrous. If we can only conduce a grateful passion of the heart, it contributes greatly to the health and happiness of every society. We should learn such lessons as would kindle in ourselves the promotion of good morals, both private and public; hence amongst the innumerable blessings, health would be much promoted by the consciousness of doing our duty, and would diffuse through the heart that habitual complacency and joy most friendly to health. No one will doubt that health is the result of nicely balanced appetites and passions.

Harmony is one of the great powers that wards off disease, both mental and corporal; without it, imperceptible strokes are given to those delicate fibres of which we are composed, until we are insensibly injured. On the other hand we are presented with all the innocent pleasures of human life, that purifies our enjoyments and renders them more grateful and generous, thus making us habitually cheerful. Cheerfulness promotes happiness and banishes many discontentments and bears the same friendly regard to the mind as to the body. Then we can look around on this vast world, where beauty and goodness is reflected from every object, where every heart glows and every comfort is sweetened by the same indulgent hand.

Thus it is that gratitude prepares a good man for the enjoyment of prosperity; for not only has he as full a relish as others, in all the innocent pleasures of life, but moreover, in these he holds communion with God. In all that is good or fair, he traces his hand. From the beauties of nature, from the improvements of art, from the blessings of public or private life, he raises his affections to the great Fountain of all happiness, which surrounds him and this widens the sphere of his enjoyments by adding to the pleasures of sense the far more exquisite joys of the heart.

This nourishes that fervent love of God and man, constituting the heart, gladdening the religion of Christ. This teaches us to deny ourselves and follow in the exercise of all virtue, wherein consists the life of religion, laying aside all idle quarrels, self-interest and needless debates about circumstantials, for this religion is not in words but in works; not in opinions but in assurances; not in speculation but in practice. It is this religion all men ought to love for their own sakes, because a holy life which it teaches gives a comfortable death and happy eternity.

CONSTITUTION.

Constitution and By-Law of the Indiana County Medical

Society, as revised and amended September 9, 1890, and approved by the Censors of the Seventh Censorial District, October 21, 1890.

TITLE OF SOCIETY—ARTICLE I.—The name and title of this society shall be The Indiana County Medical Society.

OBJECTS OF THIS SOCIETY—ARTICLE II.—The objects of this society shall be the advancement of medical knowledge, the promotion of harmony, union and friendly intercourse amongst its members, the protection of the interests, honor and usefulness of the profession, and to preserve the health and protect the lives of the community

ARTICLE III.—This society shall be subject to the rules and regulations laid down in the Sixth Article of the Constitution of The Medical Society of the State of Pennsylvania.

Organization—Section 1.—The members of the profession in any county in this State, who desire so to do, may form themselves into a county society—Provided—that the public notice of the proposed meeting for that purpose be given, and that all the regular members of the profession in the county be invited to join therein; and said Society may adopt rules for their government—Provided—the same do not contravene those of the State Society; may elect officers and do such other matters as may be necessary to carry out the objects of their Association.

Qualifications of Members—Sec. 2.—No one shall be admitted as a member of this Society unless he is either a graduate in medicine of some medical school considered respectable by this Society, or who is known by the members of this Society to have been a good respectable practitioner for twenty years, and who is known by this Society to be a regular practitioner.

Patent Medicines and Instruments—Sec. 3.—Any physician who shall procure a patent for a remedy or instrument of surgery, or who sells or deals in patent remedies or nostrums, or who prescribes a remedy without knowing its composition, or who shall hereafter give a certificate in favor of a patent remedy or instrument of surgery, or who enters into a collusive agreement with an apothecary to receive pecuniary compensation or patronage for sending his prescription to said apothecary, shall be disqualified from becoming or remaining a member of this Society.

Approval of Censors—Sec. 4.—As soon as a County Society is organized the Secretary thereof shall transmit to the Censors of the district two copies of their rules and regulations, with the names of their officers and members, and as soon as one of said copies is returned with the approval of the said Censors or a majority of them, they shall be authorized to elect one delegate to the State Society for every five of its members, and one delegate where the Society does not consist of five members, and one delegate to the American Medical Association for every ten resident members, and one additional delegate for an additional fraction of more than half that number.

Code of Ethics—Sec. 5.—Every County Society shall enforce the observance by its members the Code of Ethics adopted by the State Society, and they shall be authorized to censure or expel any member convicted of violating its provisions.

Expulsion—Sec. 6.—Any member of a County Society who is censured or expelled shall have the right to appeal to the Censors of the district any time within three months after the Society notifies him of their decision.

Rights of Consultation Suspended—Sec. 7.—Any member who is expelled shall be debarred from the rights of consultation or the privileges of professional intercourse with any member of the State Society.

Annual Reports—Sec. 8.—The County Societies shall report annually to the State Society a list of their officers and members, any new rules they may adopt and such other matter as they deem interesting.

Fee Bills—Sec. 9.—Each County Society shall have a right to fix a fee bill for regulating charges of its members for professional services.

Meetings—Sec. 10.—County Societies shall hold at least two meetings in each year, but have the privilege of holding as many meetings as they see proper.

Mutual Improvements—Sec. 11.—Each Society shall have full authority to adopt such measures as they may deem most efficient for mutual improvement, for exciting a spirit of emulation, for facilitating a dissemination of useful information, for promoting friendly intercourse amongst its members, and for the advancement of medical science.

Neglect of Duty—Sec. 12.—If any County Medical Society shall neglect to perform all such acts as may be required to be done by the laws of the State Society or which may be considered derogatory to the honor of the medical profession, or who shall oppose or neglect to comply with the laws of the State Society, such County Society, during such delinquency shall have their privileges as a portion of the State Society suspended and their delegates shall not be entitled to a seat in the State Society.

HONORARY MEMBERS—ARTICLE IV.—Sec. 1.—Honorary members may be admitted by a vote of two-thirds of the members present, who shall have a right to speak on any subject before the Society, but not to vote.

Sec. 2.—Honorary members engaged in the practice of medicine shall be required to pay the initiation fee.

OFFICERS OF THE SOCIETY—ART. V.—Sec. 1.—The officers of this Society shall be a President, Vice President, Secretary, Treasurer, three Medical Examiners and three Censors. Each officer to be elected annually by a majority vote to serve for one year or until another is elected to succeed him.

Sec. 2.—At the first election for Censors and Examiners one person shall be elected for one year, one person for two years and one person for three years for each of the offices, viz: Censors and Examiners, and one person shall be elected annually thereafter to serve for three years in the offices of Censor and Examiner.

Day of Election—Sec. 3.—All officers shall be elected by ballot and a majority vote at the regular meeting in May.

Delegates—Sec. 4.—Delegates to the Medical Society of the State of Pennsylvania and American Medical Association shall be elected annually according to the Constitution and By-Laws of those societies.

DUTIES OF MEMBERS—ART. VI.—*Attendance*—Sec. 1.—Any member of this Society living in the boroughs of Indiana, who fails to attend two regular meetings consecutively, and members outside the boroughs of Indiana who fail to attend three regular meetings of the Society consecutively shall be dropped from the list of members unless they give the Society satisfactory reasons for their absence.

Duties of Members—Sec. 2.—Any member who fails to perform any duty assigned by the Society in proportion to the duties expected and performed by the members of County Medical Societies, such as preparing and reading papers or essays on medical or surgical subjects; or attending meetings of the Medical Society of the State of Pennsylvania or American Medical Association, shall be dropped from the list of members unless they give the Society satisfactory reasons for their absence.

Candidates—Sec. 3.—Every candidate for membership shall be proposed at a regular meeting, referred to the board of Censors, who shall report at the next meeting, when a ballot may be taken.

ART. VII.—*Code of Ethics.*—This Society adopts as part of its regulations the Code of Ethics of the American Medical Association.

AMENDMENTS—ART. VII.—No addition, alteration or amendment can be made to this Constitution without the unanimous vote of the members present, but if objections be made, the addition, alteration or amendment shall lie over to the next regular meeting; when if two-thirds of the members present vote for it, it shall be adopted.

BY-LAWS.

MEETINGS—ARTICLE I.—Sec. 1.—The regular meetings of this Society shall be held in the boroughs of Indiana, on the second Tuesdays of January, May and September.

Sec. 2.—The Society may hold as many special meetings as they see proper.

Sec. 3.—The President shall call a special meeting at any time, when requested in writing by members of Society.

Sec. 4.—Five members shall always constitute a quorum.

DUTIES OF OFFICERS.—ART. II.—*President*—Sec. 1.—It shall be the duty of the President to preside at all meetings, enforce a due observance of the Constitution and By-Laws, appoint all committees, give the casting vote and perform all other duties, which by usage and custom belong to that office.

Vice President—Sec. 2.—The Vice President shall assist the President when necessary, and preside in his absence, and in the absence of both President and Vice President, the Society shall appoint a President pro tem.

Secretary—Sec. 3.—The Secretary shall keep the minutes of the proceedings of all meetings, insert the same in a book kept for that purpose when adopted, and perform such other duties asusually appertain to that office.

Treasurer—Sec. 4.—The Treasurer shall receive all monies due the Society, disburse the same as directed by vote of Society, and make a full and true report of the same at the annual meeting in May.

Duties of Censors—Sec. 5.—It shall be the duty of the Censors to inquire into the character and standing of all candidates for membership, and report on their eligibility at the next meeting of the Society, to investigate any disagreement which may occur between members, and endeavor to restore harmony if possible. When a member is charged with an infringement on the laws of the Society it shall be the duty of the Censors fully and impartially to investigate the same, and if they deem it well founded, to report the case to the Society at the next meeting with their decision..

Duties of Medical Examiners—Sec. 6.—It shall be the duty of the Medical Examiners to examine all applicants for admission as students of Medicine, under the tuition of members of this Society, and said Committee of Examiners shall withhold its certificate from any applicant unless he is of good moral character, possesses the preparatory education required by the American Medical Association, viz: A good English education, a knowledge of Natural Philosophy and the Elementary Mathematical Sciences, including Geometry and Algebra, and such an acquaintance at least with the Latin and Greek languages as will enable them to appreciate the technical language of Medicine, and read and write prescriptions correctly, and no member of this Society shall receive a student who fails to procure a certificate from the Examiners, or a diploma from a College legally entitled to confer degrees.

ELECTION OF MEMBERS—ART. III.—Sec. 1.—Application for membership shall be made to the Society at least two months before they are voted for, and if the Censors report favorably, they may be elected by a two-third vote of the members present, and on admission shall pay the sum of one dollar as an initiation fee and sign the Constitution and By-Laws. An applicant being rejected for membership, cannot apply again for the period of one year.

Offenses, Trials—Sec. 2.—If any member violates the laws and regulations of this Society: upon a charge in writing, to the Censors, it shall be their duty to notify the accused member of the same and, if after due investigation they consider the charge in writing sustained, they shall report the case to the Society at its next meeting. Notifying the accused of the same, if he fails to come forward and give the Society satisfaction, the Society shall take such action as they consider right and proper, and either suspend or expel the member according to the nature of the offense.

Expulsion requires a two-third vote.

Art. IV.—*Funds*—Funds for defraying the expenses of the Society may be raised by assessment.

Art. V.—*Papers Read*—Sec. 1.—The President shall appoint at least two essayists at each meeting of Society to prepare and read papers at the next meeting of Society, on any medical or surgical subject they may see proper to select. Members failing to comply with their appointments shall be dealt with according to the second Section of Article 6 of the Constitution.

Auditors—Sec. 2.—The President shall appoint three Auditors annually to examine and audit the Treasurer's report in May, and also appoint special committees when required.

Sec. 3.—Any rule or By-Law not covered by this list shall be regulated by Cushing's Manual of Parliamentary Practice.

Order of Business—Article VI.---The following order of business shall govern the Society:

1. Calling the roll.
2. Reading the minutes of last meeting of Society.
3. Report of special committees.
4. Any business requiring early considerations.
5. Report of the Censors.
6. Election of new members.
7. Report of the Medical Examiners.
8. Report of the Delegates to the State Medical Society.
9. Report of the Delegates to American Medical Association.
10. Written communications---Papers read and discussed.
11. Oral communications---Shall be received and discussed.
12. New members proposed.
13. Any new business may be brought forward.
14. Election of officers.
15. Unfinished and miscellaneous business.
16. Adjournment.

Amendment---Art.---These By-Laws may be suspended, altered or amended by a vote of two-thirds of the members present at any regular meeting.

PHYSICIANS' FEE BILL.

Fee Bill adopted by the Indiana County Medical Society, September 7, 1867.

PRACTICE.

Day visit in town	$1 00
Night visit in town	2 00

RATES OF MILEAGE.

A visit of one mile	2 00
" two miles	3 00
" three "	3 50
" four "	4 00
" five "	4 50
" six "	5 00
" seven "	5 50
" eight "	6 00
" nine "	6 50
" ten "	7 00
Over ten miles, per mile	1 00
Consultation, in addition to milage, optional	5 00
Mileage for night visits 50 per cent. over day visits.	
When the first visit is made to a case on Sunday, 50 per cent. additional to regular fees shall be charged, optional.	

OBSTETRICS, &c.

Natural labor	10 00
Labor by turning $15 00 to	25 00
Labor by forceps	15 00
Craniotomy	50 00
Adherent placenta	10 00
Placenta Brevia	50 00
Abortion	10 00
Uterine polypus	50 00
Imperforate hymen	25 00
Examination by vaginal speculum	2 50
Reducing ante-version of uterus	5 00
Reducing retroversion of uterus	5 00

SURGERY.

REDUCING LUXATIONS OF

Inferior maxilla	5 00
Clavicle	15 00
Shoulder	20 00
Elbow	15 00
Head of radius	10 00
Wrist	15 00
Femur	75 00
Knee	25 00
Patella	15 00
Head of fibula	10 00
Ankle	25 00
Ankle with fracture	30 00

REDUCING FRACTURE OF

Femur	20 00
Leg	15 00
Humerus	15 00
Radius	10 00
Ulna	10 00
Ribs	10 00
All other fractures of limbs	5 00

AMPUTATION OF

Arm	30 00
Shoulder joint	50 00
Elbow	50 00
Fore-arm	35 00
Wrist	30 00
Fingers, each	5 00
Hip joint	100 00
Femur	75 00
Leg	50 00
Foot	50 00

DRESSING WOUNDS

Simple incised	$2 00
All sutures	1 00

OPERATION FOR

Trephining	50 00
Cataract	25 00
Strabismus	25 00
Pterygium	35 00
Entropion	20 00
Ectropion	20 00
Fistula lachrymalis	25 00
Abscess of antrum	15 00
Extirpation of eye	50 00
Hair lip—single	25 00
Hair lip—double	50 00
Epulis	25 00
Enlarged tonsils	5 00
Staphyloraphy	100 00
Laryngotomy	100 00
Tracheotomy	100 00
Extirpation of mammary gland	50 00
Paracentesis thoracis	25 00
Paracentesis abdominis	15 00
Strangulated hernia, femoral	75 00
Strangulated hernia, inguinal	50 00
Artificial anus	25 00
Hemorrhoids	50 00
Fistula in ano	50 00
Lithatrity	100 00
Lithotomy	200 00
Castration	50 00
Hydrocele	15 00
Varicocele	50 00
Phymosis	15 00
Paraphymosis	15 00
Epispadias	25 00
Hypospadias	25 00
Urethral catheterism	2 50
Gonorrhœa	20 00
Syphlis, (one-half in adv.)	50 00
Club foot	100 00

TUMORS.

Operations for scirrhus, calloid, encephaloid, melanosis, and all other maglignant tumors, in proportion to location, &c., &c. minimum fee	25 00

LIGATION OF ARTERIES.

Carotid	$100 00
Facial	25 00
Subclavian	75 00
Axillary	50 00
Brachial	25 00
Radial	20 00
Ulnar	20 00
Iliac	100 00
Femoral	100 00

Popliteal	100 00
Posterior tibial.	50 00
Anterior	30 00
Peroneal	50 00

All necessary after treatment in obstetrical and surgical cases to be charged for at the usual rates.

POST MORTEM EXAMINATIONS.

Post mortem examination before a coroner or a magistrate, where no evidence is to be given in court	$ 50 00
Post mortem examination where evidence is to be given in court	100 00
Post mortem examination when exhumed	150 00
Post mortem examination with chemical analysis	250 00

Regular mileage to be charged in addition to the above.

MISCELLANEOUS.

Cupping in office	$ 2 00
Bleeding in office	1 00
Extracting teeth, each	50
Administering ether	1 00
Vaccination, for one in a family	1 00
Vaccination for each additional person, in a family	50

Advice in office from $1 to $5.

APPENDIX.

Regular and honorary members of this society, engaged in the practice of medicine, are required to make their charges conform to the foregoing fee bill.

When possible, all accounts are to be settled semi-annually.

Where a number of visits are made at the same time in a neighborhood, full mileage shall be charged in each case; provided that the services of a physicians cannot be dispensed with.

INDEX.

Name	Page	Name	Page
Adair, James T.	20	Devlin, Samuel F.	6
Adair, Hugh	43	Devoe, Arthur	39
Allison, David R.	56	Devoe, Marmora	39
Allison, Samuel C.	45	Dickie, Edward H.	28
Allison, Alex. H.	23	Dickeson, Henry	65
Altman, William	6	Dodson, Wm. E.	48
Annwalt, J. W.	14	Duffield, Samuel	12
Anderson, William	36	Dunwoodie, John W.	52
Andrews, Dr.	12		
Ake, Joseph H.	19	Earhart, Elias B.	60
Ansley, Wm. B.	54	Edgar, J. C.	43
Ansley, Joseph M.	54	Ehrenfedt, N. F.	38
Anthony, William	47	Elder, Samuel M.	41
Armstrong, A. H.	46	Emerson, Edward P.	11
Arney, George F.	33	Evans, John	32
		Evans, John N.	25
Bain, Dr.	59	Ewing, C. M.	29
Bair, John	46	Ewing, James R.	27
Barr, Robert	8		
Baldwin, James D.	24	Falconer, Archibald	16
Barker, John A.	60	Faulk, Henry	49
Barclay, Wm. F.	58	French, Jonathan	33
Barrett, Henry S.	63	Frederick, William	10
Barrett, Elisha D.	61	Fundenberg, Dr.	13
Barrett, Samuel D.	62		
Berryhill, Samuel G.	53	Gamble, George M.	9
Bingell, Ferdinand F.	48	Gamble, Thoedore B.	50
Bishop, J. J. J.	45	Getty, Dr.	5
Bell, James H.	21	George, Wm. J.	49
Blose, Joseph U.	20	George, M. R.	59
Bolinger, Dr.	22	Gemmill, Dr.	13
Brallier, Emanuel	20	Gettys, George W.	6
Brown, Samuel P.	12	Glasgow, George M.	26
Bryson, James A.	51	Gilpin, John	12
Buchanan, John J.	25	Gillespie, Dr.	12
Burrell, D. Dr.	33	Golden, Joseph C	24
		Goodhart, George	52
Caldwell, William	18	Green, John B.	25
Calhoun, Bruce L.	22	Gross, Augustus H.	40
Calvin, Hugh A.	63		
Campbell, Dr.	14	Hadden, John M.	30
Cameron, Norris	21	Hamill, Dr.	13
Campbell, J. Gilbert	33	Hamilton, Andrew A.	66
Cass, John T.	45	Hay, John	6
Carson, Thomas	58	Hays, George	5
Carson, John B.	17	Harding, James L.	18
Claggett, Luther S.	15	Hartwell, Dr.	30
Cantwell, Terrence J	14	Henry, Thomas J	31
Clark, A. Jackson	7	Hildebrand, Dr.	48
Cleis, George	29	Householder, M. C.	60
Crawford, Dr.	9	Hosack, William	20
Craighead, Dr.	12	Hufeland, Dr.	36
Craig, William	43	Hughes, John W.	15
Crawford, James L.	58	Hunter, William	16
Crawford, David R.	62	Hunter, George	17
Crawford, W. T.	63		
Crooks, Joseph	35	Irwin, Crawford	7
Crooks, John W.	28	Irwin, George	40
Cunningham, Wm. N.	38	Irwin, Benjamin C.	45
Davis, Thomas E.	66	Jack, William	40
Davis, James G.	42	Jackson, David P.	11
Davis, John A.	33	Jackson, Robert M. S.	12
Davison, John B.	47	Johnston, William W.	60
Davison, Thomas J	67	Johnston, Andrew	9

INDEX.

Name	Page	Name	Page
Johnston, Andrew A	11	Mitchell, Robert	34
Jones, Dr	54	Murray, Thomas	56
		Myers, Ambrose H	25
Kelly, James	20		
Kerr, Joseph M	11	Ogden, Samuel M	21
Klages, Theodore F	9	Orr, R. M	22
Kier, James A	56		
Klingensmith, I. P	16	Palmer, Dr	44
Krebs, A. Bryan	26	Parker, Wm. C	41
		Patton, James M	62
Laney, Thomas M	14	Pratt, William A	19
Larimer, William T	44	Pitman, H. B	28
Leyda, Isaac N	16	Powell, William	26
Lewis, George R	43	Purrington, Augustus F	37
Liggett, Robert	18		
Livingston, Dr	48	Rankin, D. Carson	64
Lomison, Henry G	57	Rea, Alexander M	22
Lowman, Alonza	50	Redick, Samuel T	57
Loughry, James N	45	Reed, William	37
Lovelace, R. A	19	Reed, Wm. L	33
Luke, J. B	51	Reed, Dr	5
Lydick, Joseph W	65	Reese, George J	60
		Rich, P. P	26
Mabon, Thomas	40	Ross, James	61
Mabon, James	32	Row, Herman	37
Marlin, Thomas J	22	Rutledge, S. R	15
Marshall, Robert J	12	Rutledge, Albert T	17
Martin, George	21		
Mardis, Joseph	67	Shaeffer, Samuel A	55
Marshall, David M	24	Scheffer, J	24
Marshall, Dr	30	Shields, J. Milton	24
McAdoo, Elmer E	65	Shields, Winfield S	24
McAdoo, John	52	Shields, James	32
McAfoos, Harvey F	51	Shields, Wm. Lincoln	42
McBryar, William	58	Short, James C	25
McChesney, Robert	64	Shook, James C	21
McChesney, Wm. A	64	Simpson, T. P	10
McCrea, Chalmers S	50	Simmons, Dr	12
McCartney, James S	37	Sims, William N	60
McCullough, Herman L	23	Scott, Robert K	6
McClure, James D	8	Smith, C. B	52
McClure, A. S	25	Smith, John W	30
McCune, J	30	Smith, Joseph H	50
McCurdy, J	9	Souther, A. J	9
McBeth, Joseph	18	Snowden, D. Harrold	47
McConnaughy, Robert	57	Snowden, H. S	57
McConnaughy, Frank	14	Spear, William R	14
McEwen, William	53	Sterrett, Benjamin	55
McEwen, Christopher	53	Stewart, Joseph F	40
McEwen, Joseph W	54	Stewart, James M	34
McEwen, Charles M	55	Stewart, Orlando C	23
McFarland, John	56	Stewart, Wm. G	6
McHenry, E. Q	66	Stewart, Samuel F	7
McHenry, George J	47	Stewart, Wallace B	9
McKee, Samuel	26	St. Clair, Thomas	35
McKim, Dr	13	St. Clair, Charles M	38
McGowan, William D	7	St. Clair, John M	39
McMillen, John C	25	Sturgeon, David P	39
McMullen, James	49	Swan, Samuel M	36
McMullen, Thomas	10	Swift, Elisha P	17
McNutt, John S	22	Sweeny, Barnabas	61
Miller, G. W	50		
Miller, Samuel G	68	Talmage, Samuel	3
Miller, Christopher C	41	Taylor, James	18
Miller, J. Sloan	29	Taylor, James M	35
Miller, James Calvin	21	Taylor, William S	59
Miller, Martin L	13	Thomas, Shadrach H	33
Meeker, Dr	60	Thompson, John K	37
Morgan, James	57	Tomb, Robert J	8
Morrow, J. Wilson	46	Tomb, Benjamin F	9
Morrow, James	27	Torrence, James M	38
Morrow, Wm. L	27	Tussey, A. Edgar	16
Morrison, John C	32		
Moorhead, Thomas	35	Van Antwerp, Eugene H	59

Vanhorn, Dr	5
Virtue, Samuel W	44
Wakefield, J. C	30
Walker, Wm. B	32
Wassam, Adam C	20
Wiggins, Samuel L	10
Wiley, Isaac W	13
Young, John	6
Young, Frank	5

RESOLUTION AND MEMOIRS.

Stewart, James M	71
Stewart, Joseph F	72
Adair, James T	72
Barr, Robert	73
Elder, Samuel M	73
McMullen, Thomas	74
McHenry, George	75
Indiana County Medical Society	76
Report of Indiana County Medical Society	107
Address of Wm. Anderson in accepting Presidency of the Medical Society of State of Pennsylvania	117
Address of Wm. Anderson before the annual meeting of the Medical Society of the State of Pennsylvania	118
Sclerosis of the Nerve Centres	131
Pyemia	144
Nervous Disease	154
Bacteria	163
Tobacco	172
Hygiene	178
Constitution and By-Laws of the Indiana County Medical Society	188

Physicians' Fee Bill	196

TOWNS AND TOWNSHIPS.

Armagh	5
Avonmore	10
Bells mills	10
Blairsville	11
Centerville	18
Cherrytree	19
Clarksburg	21
Cookport	23
Covode	24
Diamondville	24
Dixonville	25
Georgeville	26
Glenn Campbell	26
Gettysburg	28
Greenville	29
Homer City	32
Indiana	33
Jacksonville	40
Kimmell	42
West Lebanon	43
Marchand	45
Marion	46
Mechanicsburg	48
Newville	50
Nolo	51
Pine Flats	51
Plumville	52
Shelocta	63
Smicksburg	60
Smithport	65
Strongstown	66
Taylorsville	67
Wheatfield Township	68

ERRATA.

Page 21.—Dr. James Curry Shook graduated in 1891.

" 28.—Dr. Joseph H. Ake located at Gettysburg in 1850.

" 29.—Dr. Wallace B. Stewart spent the summer of 1858 in Nebraska.

" 32.—Homer City was laid out in 1854.

" 37.—Dr. W. B. Stewart returned to Greenville in 1856.

" " —Dr. Reed practiced with Dr. St.Clair until 1859.

" 66.—Dr. Joseph R. Golden.

" 67.—Dr. Jasper Mardis.

" 146.—Tenth line "Angeiolucitis."

www.ingramcontent.com/pod-product-compliance
Lightning Source LLC
Chambersburg PA
CBHW020927230426
43666CB00008B/1597